MASTERING MANIFESTATION

MASTERING MANIFESTATION

12 KEYS TO UNLOCK YOUR HIDDEN POTENTIAL AND LIVE THE LIFE OF YOUR DREAMS

SHANNON MACDONALD

MASTERING MANIFESTATION

BY SHANNON MACDONALD

Publication Date: August, 2021

ISBN: 978-1-7365102-2-3 (PB)

More Transformational Books by Shannon MacDonald

WWW.SHANNONMACDONALD.NET

DEDICATION

This book is dedicated in loving memory to my mother, Tonita (Aweica), who taught me to follow my heart and live my dreams, and to my husband, Carl, who reminded me how. Without them, this book would still be sleeping inside my own dream of forgetfulness.

The beauty of life is not about what we set out to accomplish. It's about how we remember to sing, dance, and play in the timeless moments of now. For in these moments, playfulness unlocks the door to imagination where our soul's purpose is remembered and our dreams are inspired to come true.

— SHANNON MACDONALD

CONTENTS

FOREWORD

BY DAVID MOREHOUSE, PH.D

Shannon is incredible, and her book walks you through some excellent steps while asking great questions to help you reach the clarity you seek. It is full of brilliant insights and tips on how to master the moment and create, no manifest the life of your dreams.

It has always been my practice to encourage others to write, objectify their thoughts, emotions, and knowledge to benefit others. Truly we only learn when we examine life through others' lenses and share our lives with others by objectifying our experiences and wisdom. I believe there is a book or books in all of us, and I am humbled to read and absorb others' knowledge.

The great challenge for those who write is to find the resonant bar of truth they will offer the reader that might help them discover answers to the great mysteries of life. One of the critical secrets we all face is that greatest of all rules for life, which is, we are only responsible for what we do in the "moment" and little else. The past is a conceptual illusion morphing at the speed of thought, faster than the speed of light. The future, yet unrealized, exists as an infinite field of unlimited possibilities. The promise and potential of attracting into the moment that which you dream or desire issues from your mastery of self in the moment, and all that entails.

Shannon understands this and offers 12 keys or steps for unlocking your hidden potential. Consider these keys tools for use in the moment. Consider these gifts to you from one who continues her work in the physical and nonphysical world where knowledge is gained. Shannon brings her knowledge together in this works pages in an intelligently organized, well crafted, and skilled manner. She understands the transformative nature of being present in the moment yet shows you how to maximize that presence by making it purposeful, meaningful, and productive. Presence without purpose is as empty as space. Seeing the world differently requires living life differently, and doing this is far easier when presented time tested and proven recipes for success and life examples as guides.

This book should be read by anyone looking for a roadmap on using our mighty mind and heart to master our life and world. If you master the 12 keys offered here, you can create the most incredible life ever. You'll learn how mind, body, spirit, and loving practice are interconnected in manifesting within the moment. You will love the step by step and find yourself reading this book repeatedly until it becomes a constant in your mind. I consider it time well spent and practice worthy of my focus.

Enjoy this journey.

David Morehouse, Ph.D.

Dr. David Morehouse is an International Best-selling Author and the world's leading teacher of Remote Viewing and Spiritual Transformation. Formerly a highly decorated special operations officer in the US Army, he is author of the international best-seller Psychic Warrior which is available in 14 languages. www.DavidMorehouse.com

ACKNOWLEDGMENT

My heart is filled with love and gratitude for every moment I have experienced, every interaction I have encountered, and every breath I have taken to lead me to the point of writing this acknowledgment. Without being present and grateful for all of these combined gifts of life, I would not be able to feel into the truth and beauty of the song of my soul as it carries the melody of the Infinite Creator within me. My first and foremost acknowledgment is honoring the love, light, and beauty of the Divine Universe as it guides me to my purpose and the destiny of my dreams.

I have countless people to honor and all circumstances to thank for bringing me to where I am today. It's impossible to acknowledge them all. I do know that the vibration of my gratitude will speak for me in ways that go beyond my written words into the hearts of whom they belong. These experiences and encounters have shaped a shy, quiet, insecure, and afraid, little girl into blooming into the grandest and most powerful vision of the divine woman I always dreamed of becoming and continue to become.

I thank my two beautiful daughters, Angela and Heidi, who chose me to be their mother in this life. They truly hold my heart with every breath they take. They have given me the gift of knowing unconditional love—the type of love that can only be known through the lens of an unfiltered heart.

I thank my father, Tom; my mother, Tonita; and my stepmother, Ruby. In their own ways, they each provided the exact foundation and formula I needed to discover my true gifts of insight, courage, perseverance, and belief.

I thank my brother, Michael, and my sister, Deborah. They gave me the gift of being a big sister as we learned to laugh, play, and cry together through the glories and tribulations of life.

I thank my best friend, Summer, for always being there, no matter what. She gave me the gift of knowing true and lasting friendship.

I thank my brother, Tim, and sister-in-law, Susan, for reminding me to have more fun and not take myself so seriously.

I thank my sister-in-law, Francesca. Her words of love and wisdom during a time of great darkness gave me the hope and vision to attract and cultivate a flourishing relationship with a partner who is now my husband.

Most of all, I acknowledge my beloved husband, Carl. Against all odds, we still managed to meet from opposite sides of the country, fall in love, and follow our hearts to create a magical life together, accelerated-style! Destiny persevered in uniting us as we listened within our hearts to the gentle and subtle calling of our souls. Truly, without him, this book would have floated through my consciousness as a fading dream of what could have been. He is the one who recognized the sleeping dream within me and sparked my memory into remembering the truth of who I am. He anchors the 12 Keys of Conscious Creation within our collective memory while holding the space for me to unlock what is already inside of me—inside of all of us. It is within our magical and synergistic relationship in which *Mastering Manifestation* is not just a book title; it is truly our life together in this giant playground of creation we call life. For that, along with his endless days and nights of editing this book with exuberance and support while fixing my continual run-on sentences, I am eternally grateful!

INTRODUCTION

Do you live the life of your dreams or just dream of the life you wish you could live?

Everyone has dreams. Not everyone knows that they have the ability to become an awakened dreamer and that dreams are one of their most precious possessions. Dreams can either be nourished or neglected, depending on your thoughts, beliefs, and emotional energy. Whether you are currently living the life of your dreams or just dreaming of the life you wish you could live, you may not be aware of how you got there. The information and messages presented in this book provide you with the roadmap. This map contains uncommonly known missing links that you can utilize to attract and create anything you truly desire to become and long to experience in the playground of your life. When you awaken within the dream of remembrance, your dreams begin to manifest outwardly from your inner reality. You begin to become the awakened dreamer of your destiny versus the blind follower of your fate.

In Part III of this book, the *12 Keys of Conscious Creation* reveal the secrets to unlock your hidden potential and live the life of your dreams. Each Key is necessary and unique in its function to help you consciously and powerfully become your own master of manifestation in life. They gracefully flow through the currents of inner reality to attract, create, and sustain the life of your dreams. The inspiration of your imagination, the focus of your thoughts, and the energy of your highest emotions are the gurus of your own enlightened wisdom as you awaken within the dream of remembrance.

Everything starts with a thought, but not every thought becomes actualized into reality until it has been successfully united within the energy of your feelings and emotions. By learning how to focus the energy of your thoughts and raise the energy of your emotions, dreams that have been lying dormant will be awakened. Only then can you step into a new reality that transcends old beliefs of limitation and self-sabotaging patterns.

If you are already living the life of your dreams (and are truly living the life of your dreams, not someone else's expectations of their dreams for you), then you already must know this on some level, and the 12 Keys of Conscious Creation within this book will be an affirmation of your remembrance. If you are still just dreaming of the life you wish you could live or dreaming of the things you wish you could have, be, or do, then this book will help you reestablish your connection to the raw materials you already own in order to attract and create your heart's desires into the most joyful, inspired, and purposeful story within the playground of your life.

PREFACE

My Dreams are *who I am.*

Everything about me and who I think I am boils down to one primary thing: my dreams. As a child, I always wanted to fly. I spent countless hours daydreaming about how to accomplish this. Even though people, circumstances, and experiences said otherwise, I still maintained a deep knowing that our physical bodies and potentials are so much more than what we are told, see, and ultimately believe. I held an inherent knowing that our beliefs keep us within a dream of limitation, and from what we are truly capable of doing, being, and becoming.

After several summers of bravely or foolishly (you decide), yet unsuccessfully, attempting to fly off the top of our shed in the backyard, I found myself disillusioned. Maybe the dreams I believed in did not exist after all. Perhaps the *grown-ups* were right, and flying was just a silly fantasy. Maybe I needed to concentrate on achievable things, like getting good grades, riding a bike, or playing an instrument.

After about three or four summers of flapping my "wings" and jumping off the shed, only to land harshly and painfully on the ground, did I once and for all sorrowfully declare that I could not fly. I was heartbroken, and my dream was shattered. I placed the broken pieces in a box and buried it deep inside of me.

I spent my remaining summers as a child cultivating my daydreams. No longer attached to the fantasy of flying off the shed, I was free to explore my inner playground through reading, writing poems, and connecting with nature. This was my sanctuary, where I found solace, joy, freedom, and refuge.

Several years older than my siblings and in a neighborhood with few kids my age, I often found myself alone. My imagination would lead me on grand adventures as I sat outside in communion with nature. I opened my heart to the flowers, trees, birds, and squirrels and simply *listened* to what they had to tell me. During these years, I discovered that everything is alive and has something to say. All I needed to do was be still and listen for the unspoken language to be heard within me. I also learned that nothing is as it seems and there is a deeper truth to many things we are told to believe. I opened my heart to the vibrations of beauty and kindness and discovered these qualities are the ultimate by-products of love. I learned that we are all connected to an infinite Source and that everything I did, thought and felt was a part of the whole that affected everything else.

Through all of my lessons in life, I have come to know that anything is possible and that the outcome of possibility is simply tied to our thoughts, feelings, and beliefs. Of course, as a child, I did not comprehend this insight as I am able to do now. I also learned countless lessons, as one would say, the hard way. Nevertheless, my dreams, as well as my lessons, became a part of me and have sculpted who I am today. While sometimes changing, my dreams absorbed into my inner knowing and gave me the hope and inspiration to believe I could fly.

I began to realize that flying meant so much more than the mere physical act. Over the years, I learned how to connect to my higher self and visit places I would never have been able to physically go. During my meditative visions as a child, my future self would often visit me to provide guidance, support, and calming reassurance during periods of deep loneliness and heartbreak. As an adult, this has come full circle as I meditate with an open and loving heart on my younger self and graciously send her the love, reassurance, and guidance she longs for.

My childhood self reminds me of the magic of dreams. She reminds me that I *can* fly. I provide her with the confidence and support she needs to continue believing in the magic of her dreams. Now, as a grown woman, I am occasionally visited by my future (much older) self in my meditative visions. Wise, confident, loving, and beautiful, she reminds me and guides me along my journey of following my heart and living my dreams.

It is within the song of our souls and the fulfillment of our dreams in which we make the most significant impact upon uplifting, improving, and healing, not only for ourselves but for our world. I remember that my dreams are who I am, and they are attracted to me as I awaken from the dream of forgetfulness and listen to the song of my soul.

ABOUT DIVINITY SPEAKS

The information shared in this book is an inspired compilation of wisdom that has been silently speaking to me for many years, from the truth of the Universe to the acceptance of my heart.

Most of the quotes in this book, unless specified, include inspirational messages from a Higher Consciousness that I simply refer to as Divinity Speaks.

I deeply believe we are all intimately connected with and have open access to Higher Consciousness. You may wish to interchange the names or labels that I use for the Divine with whichever names that suit your personal comfort level. Labels are something we use in our world of verbal and written language to help us relate to, or describe the nature of something, whether it is an idea, object, life-form, the Universe, or God. Labeling allows our minds to place the item into a specific category or classification. It helps us grasp the image of the idea, person, or thing in the mind's eye, as we simultaneously feel what this label means to us personally. The truth of the matter is that there is no universally agreed-upon name for the infinite intelligence of the Universe, and there isn't a name for the ever-present, all-knowing expression of All That Is.

The truth and wisdom of Divinity speaks to each one of us. We hear the subtle messages speak from within as we are awakened to remember and called to serve. We all have a divine destiny, and we all have a personal truth. The key is remembering how to open our hearts in order to reclaim and know this truth so that we may consciously magnetize, create, and live our happiest, healthiest, most purposeful, and inspired lives.

The insights and wisdom for the creation of this book originated from the following four paragraphs that I received as a series of inspired messages in July 2015. Little did I know then that a book would be written from the profound truth contained within this one message. In fact, it was not until this book was 95 percent written that I found this message in one of my journals. The divine wisdom within this message has been silently and unknowingly shaping my life and leading me to attract and live the life of my dreams through what I call *the secret of attraction energy*. Reading the message after four years of not giving it a conscious thought affirmed my belief that we are all divinely inspired and guided, and there is much truth in divine timing. We can become the masters of our own manifestations, and our dreams can be fulfilled once we allow our hearts to listen to love and our minds to follow our hearts.

The Highest Truth

The Universal Laws of Light and Love are one and the same. The way to access those Laws is deeply embedded inside of you. No reaching outward. Only looking inward. Inward to where you find your ease. It is the release of everything that does not serve you, which brings you to the destiny of your dreams.

Let your conscious mind flow to be at one with the body of Eternal Knowing. This is where your body, your life, becomes your creation. No duality exists here. Only accessing what feels joyous in you—or what does not feel joyous in you.

Many in your society believe creation is a function of your thoughts as in the Law of Attraction. The thoughts and words are a powerful component of your magnetism, for thoughts and words create a feeling always based on either love or fear. The manifestation lies in the attraction to the feeling as an individual and a collective. This is the Secret of Attraction Energy. This is the highest truth.

The channel through your heart is the one you are designed to listen to. The Information flows effortlessly as long as you do not allow your thoughts to interfere. What you do with this Intelligence is the consequence of your beliefs. When your beliefs align with the knowing of The Universe, your destiny is born into reality. Choose your beliefs wisely and guide them only with a loving heart.

— *DIVINITY SPEAKS*

TO THE READER

My Dream Seed

We may not have met in person, but we do know each other. As long-lost friends who celebrate when they are reunited, we are here to awaken within our collective dream of remembrance.

Dreams are like seeds planted in the garden of our realities. They need to be nourished with our attention and watered with our love. Dreams left untended will be overrun by the weeds of our fears and the neglect of our awareness.

My dream seed for your journey through your dream of remembrance is that you realize your happiness and remember your truth. May your life be fully expressed and experienced from the love within your heart and the inspiration of your dreams. May your destiny call forth your highest purpose, deepest peace, and greatest joy.

We all carry dream seeds within us. Yours is just waiting to be noticed and nourished as it bursts forth as the most beautiful garden within the song of your soul.

All my love to you, dreamer. Remember, you got this!

With love, light, beauty, and truth,

Shannon MacDonald

> *"The road of your destiny is paved by the joy of your now. Live from your heart, and see your dreams manifest into the glorious creations of your soul. Light, love, and beauty will illuminate the way to the path of your potential and the outcomes of your dreams."*
>
> — *DIVINITY SPEAKS*

PART I

THE AWAKENED DREAMER

"Listen for Me. I call to you every day. My Voice flows through your inner stillness, merges with your heart, and becomes one with your being. As your listening becomes knowing, you can hear Me more clearly. My eternal love for you is felt as your joy. As you follow your heart, you know that the truth of your own presence and the beauty of your light will guide the way to that of which you dream."

— *DIVINITY SPEAKS*

1

AWAKENING FROM THE DREAM OF FORGETFULNESS

> *Look beyond what you think you see. Look through the eyes of your Soul. The Universe is calling for your awakening.*
>
> — *DIVINITY SPEAKS*

Somewhere along the way during your journey through life, you began to remember. In this remembrance, you became aware that your life is sacred. You awakened to something that felt so real it made you question everything you thought you knew and were taught and told. It even made you question who you were and whether you were truly happy or were simply living someone else's version of happiness. All the overachieving, self-denial, and people-pleasing left you feeling as though your life were no longer your own. The endless to-do lists and the frantic running from here to there to get it all done (whatever *it* is), prompted you to question the meaning of it all and the power *it* held over you. Then, one day, the world felt different. You heard a familiar sound calling to you from deep within. You began to remember there is a world of true meaning and infinite possibilities. You began to remember that you have the freedom to choose to remain asleep in the dream of forgetfulness, or awaken to the dreams within the song of your soul.

THE SONG OF YOUR SOUL

This is not just my story. It may also be your story, and the story of many others who have forgotten how to listen to the song of the soul—the melody that echoes from deep within and throughout every moment of becoming truly present with the dreams of your destiny.

As a wife and young mother of two beautiful daughters in the 1990s, I had a life that I deeply loved and was grateful for. Even though I chose and cherished the life I lived, I neglected to honor the deepest part of my identity. I forgot what I needed to honor my path as an individual. Yes, I did say *individual*. Throughout my years of conditioning and people-pleasing, I began to pretend it was okay to put myself last. I thought it was okay to not follow my dreams or creative destiny, as long as everyone else was happy and healthy. I would tell myself that my personal happiness and growth were not as important as the happiness of others and that I could find or achieve this later. Eventually, I began to believe my own dream of forgetfulness as I chose to not follow my heart or listen to the song of my soul.

> *The song of your Soul is heard through the channel of your heart. When you listen to this melody, you will know that every moment is Divinity in creation.*
>
> — *DIVINITY SPEAKS*

THE DREAM OF REMEMBRANCE

I am reminded of the lyrics of a song, "I'm in a Hurry (and Don't Know Why)" by Alabama, which echoed throughout my dream of forgetfulness for many years. This song is about the pressures we put on ourselves to keep up with the demanding pace of modern life as we perpetually race against the clock in order to accomplish *it all*. To top it off, the song portrays the fact that one does not know why he or she is in such a hurry because the fun is taken out of life when doing so.

For years, I would actually sing this song as a type of unconscious identification as I rushed through my day to frantically get all of the things done I thought I needed to do for my family, my job, and various other obligations. It is as if I were sleepwalking through life and didn't even know it.

I began to feel like a gerbil running around on the same wheel day after day with no objective other than hurrying to accomplish my ever-growing daily *to-do* list. Don't get me wrong. I deeply loved my family and counted my blessings every day. My heart was filled with joy and gratitude as I diligently carried out my role as a wife and mother while ensuring everyone's needs were met. I obtained my RN license while managing a household with two toddlers to contribute financially to my family and fulfill my personal development. My husband was supportive of my endeavors, and even throughout the trials and tribulations of our unbalanced marriage, I felt loved.

With all the positive things I was experiencing, I began to feel there was something wrong, and there was something more. I began to feel as if everyday life was not giving me the sense of satisfaction or purpose I thought it should. I couldn't put my finger on it, and I even felt guilty that I had such feelings. Even though I was happy, I didn't feel complete. I realized there was an aspect of myself that I had been ignoring as it silently called me to wake up from the dream of forgetfulness and listen to my long-lost dream of remembrance.

Up to this point, I had not been able to see that my perpetual rushing through life, and ignoring the communication from my heart was not allowing me to feed my soul or my spiritual growth and purpose. I was also completely unaware of the fact that I could accomplish anything or become fulfilled while slowing down and feeling peaceful.

When I began to wake up, I became present with the beauty of honoring my life by slowing down. I'll provide more on that later. Little by little, I gradually discovered the Keys of Conscious Creation (*The Keys*) included in this book. I began to see how all of the rushing through life and worrying about what I could not accomplish was the exact *energy* I was *attracting*. It was this energy that kept me on the perpetual wheel of running in place and not getting anywhere.

Even though I didn't want it to be—or at least I thought I didn't want it to be, the Alabama song was my mantra. Little did I know that I got exactly what I attracted throughout those years of *unconscious* creation. This continued until I began to remember the truth of who I am, which my mind had so unknowingly forgotten. I began to replace the "I'm in a Hurry" song with the song of my soul. I believe you are reading this book right now because you are also ready to listen to the song of your soul, and you are beginning to remember.

THE AWAKENING

Remembering is a pivotal first step. As the foundation that supports all the Keys, remembering is the first of many steps up the ladder to becoming the master of your manifestations. It is like awakening from a deep and dreamless sleep and stepping into a new, but somehow familiar world you have never before seen but always felt was there. This world is a place ready to bloom into the grandest version of who you have always wanted to be and what you have always wanted to create. You begin to remember on a soul level that you are really ready to awaken to your purpose and live the life of your dreams. You begin to remember that your life is not just one big to-do list that has you frantically and continually running day after day while never feeling like you get anywhere.

This book was not written for you. It was written by you. Within the unseen energy of your highest desires are your purpose and dreams waiting to be revealed as they gently call to your heart and wait patiently for you to listen.

There is no knowledge, wisdom, or information in the universe that does not already contain an aspect of you. You are an energetic vibration encoded within the truth of the universe that always was and always will be. Intertwined within this collective consciousness is your individual ability to transcend the deep and dreamless sleep of life.

Once you begin to remember the beauty and truth of who you are as a conscious creator, you embody the secret of attraction energy. You remember the mastery and limitless potential within you as you awaken from the deep sleep of forgetfulness into your highest purpose and the life of your dreams. What you have been searching for or felt was missing is right here, right now. It's time to wake up and stop hitting snooze!

THE CONSCIOUS CREATOR

You become the master of your own creations by remembering the truth of who you are.

— *DIVINITY SPEAKS*

I must make one point clear before we proceed. Learning to master manifestation through conscious creation does not mean you must change everything about your life. It doesn't mean that you have to leave relationships or become a rebel without a cause. It does mean that you will evolve into the highest and best version of who you are meant to be and what you are designed to do and experience.

Embracing the song of your soul includes the remembrance that *your* life is sacred and that your life is merely a byproduct of your intentions, thoughts, beliefs, energy, and actions.

By reading this book, you have made an unspoken agreement with yourself, as well as with the Universe, that you are ready. At the very least, you are intrigued and open to the possibility of discovering a *new way of being a new you.* I am talking about stepping into the you and experiencing the life of your most cherished ideals, dreams, and purpose. This *you* doesn't need to be a fantasy, and your most cherished dreams don't need to feel unachievable— unless you *believe* them to be.

There is a proven and reproducible method for success that includes how you are thinking *and* feeling at this moment right now. For it is in this exact moment when the master key to unlock your greatest hidden potential is found within the uncommonly known secret of attraction energy.

WISDOM OF THE AGES

Before we proceed, I want to tell you the secret *before* the secret. The 12 Keys for success behind conscious creation are not really a secret. However, they do represent the unrealized potential and wisdom of the ages accessible to everyone right now, not sometime in the future. This is something that has always been and always will be for those who are open and willing to believe.

The inspiration, ideas, and Keys in this book emanate from the wisdom and collective enlightenment of many teachers who have gone before us. In reality, it was never really theirs or mine at all. However, it is free and available to those who have been awakened to remember, and called to share. The information belongs to *everyone* as fundamental Keys for unlocking the doors to the right kind of energy to support conscious creation. After reading this book, you will have the information and tools that millions of other people yearn to discover behind the success of attracting, creating, living, and sustaining the life of your dreams.

WHAT IS A BELIEF?

> *You see reality through the eyes of your beliefs. As you believe, so you perceive.*
>
> — *DIVINITY SPEAKS*

The only thing that I ask is to keep your mind open to the ideas presented, and reserve your judgment until you have finished reading this book. New information and new ideas can sometimes feel startling, especially if they challenge your current beliefs. We have all been born into a world that continually programs how we believe and what we should believe from childhood on. It is easy and normal to take on a belief, because that is how your parents, teachers, friends or society thinks.

You may not stop to question that a belief is only a belief, because you have accepted it as so.

In actuality, you *believe* your beliefs. But have you ever stopped, even for a minute, to think about how your beliefs came to be? Most of us never think about this until there is a condition, a situation, or an event that jolts us into reevaluating our views or position on life.

Whether they are personal, cultural, political, religious, or otherwise, our views are rarely reevaluated. Most of the time, we are not even consciously aware of where our beliefs came from. We seldom put any thought or question into if our beliefs are really our own. Perhaps our beliefs are merely formulated from something we have been told or how we have been conditioned and programmed, and now we hold them as our truths.

Maybe you have been holding onto a belief that no longer serves you. Maybe you are not even aware of this because you have not allowed yourself to open your mind to another possibility. Perhaps you hold a belief because it has not entered your thoughts that there may be other ways to believe that better suit your personal relationship with life.

As you read the information presented in this book, pay close attention to how your body *feels*. There will be more on this later, but now is a good time to start paying attention to the silent, but powerful, energy that signals you from within.

BELIEF AND KNOWING

Beliefs are barriers to the truth of Reality.

They shape your destiny as they place limitation on creation.

Question your beliefs.

Ask if they are true.

Ask if they serve you.

Ask if they bring you closer to or further away from Inner Peace.

Ask if they unite or divide families, communities, and people of the world.

Ask if they bring love or fear.

Ask if they bring peace or war.

Ask if they bring compassion or judgment.

Ask if they bring forgiveness or hatred.

Ask if they bring acceptance or intolerance.

Ask if they bring gratitude or expectation.

Ask if they serve the hearts of humankind or feed the distortion of ego.

Ask if they originate from within you or something outside of you.

When you can answer these questions without thought through the presence of Love in your heart, you will know the difference between belief and knowing.

> *Know that all beliefs are human-made. They are here to serve you or not serve you. In the end, they do not care. They are indifferent to all outcomes.*
>
> *Knowing is the truth of the Soul and the Reality within.*
>
> *Knowing holds the answers you seek and the healing of the world.*
>
> *Knowing breaks the chains of fate and unites you with your destiny.*
>
> *Knowing is the Light, the Truth, and the Way to the infinite, eternal, ever-present Reality of All That Is.*
>
> *Knowing is the remembrance of who you are as Divinity within the song of your Soul.*
>
> — DIVINITY SPEAKS

WHAT ARE DREAMS?

You have heard it said before that one person's dream could be another person's nightmare. Maybe it isn't actually a nightmare, but all dreams are unique to the individual to whom they belong. This holds true regardless of the other people in your life you choose to share your dreams with. Yes, I did say *choose*, even if you think you didn't.

Maybe you dream of a house in the country, a condo in the city, a successful and fulfilling career, a comfortable retirement, or an extravagant vacation with your spouse. Maybe you dream of finding your soulmate, having children, being healthy, or being in the best physical shape of your life. Maybe at this point in life, your dreams are being able to pay your rent and have enough money left over to buy food and clothing for your children, and put gas in your car. Maybe you dream of finishing your master's degree or completing your GED.

In order to reveal our dreams, we need to understand what they are, and from where they originate:

- Dreams (not fleeting wishes or wants) are our deepest, most heartfelt desires combined with our most inspired moments of imagination.

- While some dreams may have been carried over from our thoughts yesterday, they are only alive and active in our thoughts today.

- Dreams are either the most powerful or the most powerless in this moment right now, depending on many factors you will discover in this book.

- Dreams come in all shapes and sizes. No dream is too big or too small, and they are unique to the individual to whom they belong.

- Dreams can intertwine gracefully together on the dance floor of our imaginations, as they take us on a journey deep into our hearts and echo from our souls.

ESSENTIALLY, DREAMS ARE OUR DEEPEST DESIRES AND IMAGINATION IN FREE AND CONSTANT MOTION. THEY HAVE UNRESTRICTED ACCESS TO THE GENESIS OF CREATION THROUGH OUR BELIEFS AND PREDOMINANT ENERGY.

We can choose to be guided by our dreams, or we can choose to ignore them. Once we begin to *listen* to our hearts, *believe* in the power of our inspired imaginations, and *feel* the outcomes as our embodied truths, our dreams become supercharged magnets that begin to attract the conditions, things, and situations we most desire.

Whatever your dreams are, the important key is knowing that dreams are different for everyone. It is also important to remember that your dreams can change at any given moment, depending on the current flow of energy in which your attention is focused. We do not need to be locked into one specific dream, and we shouldn't feel like we are failures for choosing another dream. We can also have multiple dreams simultaneously. There is no limit, and there is no rule that says we must continue to hold onto the same dream today that we had five years ago, or even yesterday. When a dream changes, you are not really giving up anything except your attachment to one specific outcome that may no longer serve you.

Attachments to a specific end goal, or a specific way of reaching that goal, are like limitations in the infinite ocean of dreams. They do not allow you to gracefully flow within the multiple streams of inspiration, possibility, and outcome. As you allow a dream to change or evolve, you are merely redesigning the formula to specifically attract your new heart-inspired desires. You are, in fact, following the signs we all have access to once we remember to look, listen, trust, and feel.

Living the life of your dreams and being the *you* that you have always dreamed of being, is completely within your grasp, once you learn to be in the flow of your truest self. The best part about this is that the process is not work. The key to this is the secret of attraction energy and *remembering* how to consistently apply it to your life.

PASSION AND PURPOSE

Inside of you is a passion so great and a purpose so strong there is nothing in the Universe that can destroy it. Passion and purpose can, however, disappear from your current perception of reality, if you choose to focus elsewhere. While it is not destroyed, it simply lies dormant until your heart reminds you it is still alive.

As you become more aware of your Wisdom within, passion and purpose grows and blooms inside of you, as long as you continue to feed it with your love and care for it with your devotion. When you don't listen to your heart and don't cultivate your passion, you are unable to live the dreams of your destiny, as they become overrun by the multitude of weeds in the garden of your creation.

— DIVINITY SPEAKS

2

AWAKENING FROM FAILURE

> *Failure is only a perception in the mind. It has no bearing on the validity of your efforts or the outcome of your obstacles.*
>
> — *DIVINITY SPEAKS*

Have you ever really thought about the word *failure*? How do you feel after reading that word? Many people believe that failure means not completing or attaining something they wanted or expected to achieve, do, or have. Some believe being a failure means they are unsuccessful in life, love, health, wealth, relationships, career, and so on. For many, it leads to feelings of unworthiness, inadequacy, and self-doubt. This ultimately leads to a breakdown in faith or a breakdown of the belief that good things can or will happen. If failure occurs too many times, the majority of people will simply give up. Some people become so apathetic and broken down that they just don't care anymore, and then they start forming a belief that they just have bad luck or good things don't happen to them. It can lead to a perpetual cycle of doom and gloom, while feeling like the world is always against you, instead of conspiring for you. I would be surprised if you haven't experienced feeling like this sometime in your life, if even for a few moments, hours, or possibly days. Some people live a whole lifetime perceiving themselves as failures.

The good news is that it's not a failure to feel your emotions as you perceive something in your life as a failure. The only misfortune is not overcoming the belief that so many hold on to. The belief that failure is something real that has control over you or defines your life. It does not.

In my world, failure is not a term I utilize or even believe in. Over the years, I have learned how to look at what others may perceive as failure as just another opportunity to practice the secret of attraction energy. It is not something I remembered overnight, and it doesn't mean that I still don't have my moments of self-doubt. It is a knowing that has always been deep inside of me and that I believe is like a sleeping giant inside of us all. Once that knowing inside of me was awakened from its deep sleep of forgetfulness, I began to remember that the things I once looked at as failures were actually the things or situations that taught me my greatest lessons in life. These are the thing that shaped me into the person I am today.

The concept of failure (what I now call perceived obstacles or guideposts) is not about making myself sick from worry, guilt, regret, doubt, or hopelessness. It is not about giving up on my goals or dreams simply because something inside me says I can't do this or have that or be this or go there. It's not about complaining, pointing fingers, or feeling victimized, jealous, insecure, or angry. It's also not about starting over by doing the same thing, or by thinking the same thoughts, feeling the same way, and hoping to get different results. In fact, it is quite the opposite.

When I come to a crossroad or a perceived obstacle and don't know where to go, what to do, or how to get there, I remind myself that this is the best opportunity to push the reset button, as I surrender to the expectation of outcome. I am also reminded to forgive myself or others who may be involved in the crossroad of my perceived obstacle. I get the opportunity to learn from the experience and simply try again. Trying again means consistently maintaining the correct thoughts, feelings, and actions in order to attract the outcome I really, really want, regardless of my perceived obstacles.

In some cases, trying again could be as simple as modifying your original dream to one that better suits you today instead of yesterday. Notice I used the word *modify*. The dream may still be desired, but maybe some of the aspects or details of the dream have now changed. Maybe your dream home has changed from a beach in Hawaii to the mountains in Colorado. This is a basic example, but being attached to one specific outcome is where many can get stuck. We get stuck in a rut of not allowing the intelligence of our hearts to be in harmony with the Grand Universe to guide us toward our hearts' desires.

If something that I really, really want to achieve, have, be, do, experience, or create seems to get blocked at every crossroad, then that is my cue that I am not in the flow with the *right kind* of energy that is needed to attract and support my desired outcomes or creations in my life. This is a perfect time for a reevaluation. During this evaluation process, I may find that I am too attached to a specific way that the dream *should* manifest. I may be too attached to one particular outcome. Maybe my life has changed, and I am holding onto a dream that I wanted yesterday. The evaluation process may reveal that this dream (or portions of the dream) may no longer serve me today.

You would be surprised how often this happens during the course of life. Some people dream that their world looks and feels exactly like it did in the past. When the inevitable impossibility of this occurs, dreams become distant memories that reside in the broken hearts of unfulfilled lives. There is no shame in checking in with yourself to reevaluate what it is you think you want. At that time, ask your heart if that will bring you closer to, or further away from your true happiness and purpose in life. For in all reality, isn't that what it's all about anyway?

Achieving successful outcomes for anything in my life is about slowing down, listening to my heart, and following the signs along the way. This is a simple, yet sacred process that helps me remember and reconnect to my purpose and personal story of life. It is also about taking the *want* out of wanting, as want implies having a need that is unfulfilled. It is also about allowing instead of trying, which is something I will explain later in this book. Wanting and trying are both energies of lack, and are not the kind of energies that attract the outcomes that I desire most. That is my cue to remember to have faith and believe that my dream is already met with the conviction of truth in my heart. It's really so simple, but as humans, we seem to need to make everything so complicated.

ATTACHMENT TO OUTCOMES

Life is dynamic and ever changing. It continually flows within the fluctuating currents of destiny and desire. It is much like a river continuing its journey downstream to the ancient oceans of time. The boulders, logs, and other obstacles will eventually allow the water pass. The same is true with the energy of life as it continues on its journey of infinite possibilities, in which only time can measure, and outcomes are observed. Being too attached to *one* specific outcome can actually be a barrier to your ultimate success and happiness. I will address this in more detail later, but for now, the key to this is to remember the following:

THE UNIVERSE ALWAYS DELIVERS. IT CONSPIRES *FOR YOU* BASED ON YOUR LEVEL OF ENERGY IN EVERY MOMENT OF NOW.

The right kind of energy will find you, follow you, and flow through you, as you begin to practice and master the 12 Keys outlined in this book. This, my friends, is my world, and it can be your world too! I am saying this with the utmost sincerity and love. Nothing can stop you except your own beliefs and unwillingness to look beyond the curtain of fear and limitation, into the infinite possibilities of inspired creation, through the limitless power of attraction energy.

LISTENING TO YOUR HEART

The channel through your heart is the one you are designed to listen to.

— *DIVINITY SPEAKS*

I often assume people know what I mean when I say, "Listen to your heart." I'm sure that most have the fundamental understanding that it refers to paying attention to how you feel about something in any given situation. That is a big component of listening to your heart. How we feel about anything is a silent communication from deep within ourselves that we often refer to as our intuition.

YOU CAN CONSIDER YOUR INTUITION AS AN UNSEEN EXCHANGE OF ENERGY AND INFORMATION FROM AN EVER-PRESENT FIELD OF CONSCIOUSNESS THAT IS RECEIVED BY SENSES OTHER THAN THE THINKING BRAIN.

If you imagine your body as an antenna, and your heart as a receiver, then consciousness is the intelligent information that is broadcast in between. When we listen to our hearts, what we are doing is feeling the pure energy from our higher selves or Higher Consciousness that bypasses the conditioned mind, (our beliefs). It speaks directly to that place of knowingness inside of us that we frequently refer to as our hearts. In today's fast-paced modern society, our sense of heartful listening and intuitive guidance is easily ignored or dismissed; or it lands on the deaf ears of the conditioned mind.

Our intuition is what tunes into the unseen energetic signals or information from Higher Consciousness. As I mentioned earlier, there are countless other names for this consciousness, which I often interchange with names such as the Universe, Source Energy, Infinite Intelligence, Divinity, and God. You may have your own unique name for It, as there is no complete agreement in our physical world on the name for Higher Consciousness. One thing most will agree on with absolute scientific certainty is that there is a correlation between consciousness and our physical, material world.

THE QUANTUM FIELD

Modern science is studying the effects of how the human energy field can interact and influence the quantum field all around us. Our thoughts, emotions, beliefs, and intentions are a part of our human bio-magnetic, energetic fields that are continually communicating with the quantum field. This quantum field is not only around us, but also within us.

One of the fundamental principles of quantum physics is that as observers, we are personally involved in the creation of our own realities and that new science is beginning to reveal that the Universe is a mental construction. The Law of Attraction, in a similar fashion, means that everything that comes into your life and everything you experience is done so through the magnetic power of energy, including your thoughts. Of course, this Law of Attraction provides a foundation for this book in which the secret of attraction energy builds upon.

> ***MAGNETIZING YOUR POTENTIALS***
>
> *You think you create by your actions. But actions are only the end result of the dominoes you have put into place. They are the final pieces before the physical manifestation occurs.*
>
> *Actions are important, but the creation begins with your thoughts and the knowing of your spirit. In this knowing, there is a feeling. Depending on the outcomes of your creations, your feelings flow within a spectrum of infinite possibilities.*
>
> *The spectrum is also one of your own creation, and in turn, has its own vibrations of resonance or dissonance and stability or chaos.*
>
> *As your body feels the vibrations of your attraction, and translates them through thought, you magnetize potential outcomes, which may involve actions.*
>
> *There are times when there is no need for actions—when the vibration is in harmonic resonance with*

the energy of your love or fear; desire or despair. This cycle is repeated for everything in life.

You choose what you think, attract, feel, and create. There is no good or bad, right or wrong; there is only creation.

— *DIVINITY SPEAKS*

PART II

THE SECRET OF ATTRACTION ENERGY

"Your present moments of now are living energetic magnets. As your moments build and you turn experience into belief, and belief into feeling a certain way, your reality is likewise attracted into creation. You become how you feel from one moment to the next."

— *DIVINITY SPEAKS*

3

ENERGY, IMAGINATION, AND ANCIENT TRUTH

I Am the Source of your dreams and the Truth of your imagination.

— *DIVINITY SPEAKS*

According to modern science, as well as ancient wisdom, there is a field of intelligence that is all around us as a network that exists throughout the Universe. This field is an infinite, dynamic, and interconnected web of energy and information. As humans, we are not excluded from this network, but on the contrary, we are very much a part of this ever-present unified field.

What you or I prefer to call this intelligence is not important and in no way will alter or affect your ability to understand and follow the Keys and see their results. As I mentioned earlier, names are something we seem to need as human beings in order to label things. We do this so we can communicate with each other through our system of verbal and written language. Unfortunately, through this communication system, the original meanings of what we individually know or feel become reduced and divided throughout humanity, as personal belief systems begin to collide and disagree with the many names of Divinity. Maybe that was the grand design for our human experience. But just for a while, I would like to ask you to put aside all of the labels and names, as we explore the truth and power of Consciousness behind the curtain.

EVERYTHING IS ENERGY

There is a vibratory frequency that corresponds to *everything* in the Universe, including us. Science shows us that our bodies, as well as everything we see and don't see, exist as pure energy. This energy, which is expressed in waveform, vibrates at one frequency or another. As energetic beings, we emit and attract energetic frequencies. These frequencies either harmonize, and result in order and balance (coherence), or dis-harmonize, and result in disorder and imbalance (incoherence). There is also an infinite number of possibilities in between. What this means is that *we* have the amazing opportunity to *attract* the frequencies of energy that *we* emit in order to balance and harmonize our minds and bodies. This harmonization or coherence is a critical component in attracting the right kind of energy or the desired energy, which ultimately helps us reach our greatest potentials mentally, emotionally, physically, and spiritually. All of this helps to magnetize and create the lives of our dreams by raising our vibratory frequencies.

Wherever you are in life right now, regardless of how it appears to be, you always have the ability and opportunity to raise your vibratory frequency, or your vibration. You always have the ability and opportunity to break the chains of fate, and unite with the magnificence and wonders of your destiny. The 12 Keys of Conscious Creation in Part III are your road map to successfully access these wonders inside of you, that are just waiting to burst forth. As you begin your journey to your destiny, an important thing to remember is to remain conscious with your thoughts, speech, and emotions. Roadblocks are created through waves of negativity, self-doubt, hopelessness, and fear. There are tools and techniques to use to help raise your vibration. Some of these include meditation, mantra, music, singing, and doing things that bring you into the higher vibrations of joy, peace, purpose, and compassion. You have your own unique way. Find that and listen within.

THE KEY TO UNLOCKING UNLIMITED POSSIBILITY

As humans, we have the ability to learn, reflect, reason, apply knowledge, and feel. These qualities can help us reach beyond our current beliefs and the habitual programming of society. They also help us navigate our innate capacity to exchange information with the network of Infinite Intelligence in which we all have access. The information comes to us in the form of *thoughts and feelings,* and holds the *key* to unlocking *unlimited possibilities* in our lives. Instead of being victims of circumstance, we can learn how to clear the path of programming, and become conscious creators of our most inspired and desired lives. The path is cleared as we learn to listen from within. The more we listen from within, the more we remember *how* to live our lives on purpose as we navigate the waters of manifestation through our thoughts, feelings, and emotions.

Listen within your Soul. Your Soul lives beyond the limits of your body. Your Soul is not something you talk to or consult with, as if talking to another person you perceive to be outside of you. Your Soul is not a mere reflection of who you are or what you think. Your Soul is the endless and limitless actu-

> *ality of your expression. When you listen "to" your Soul, you are still living in the illusion of separateness, distance, space, and time. Listen within your Soul and know you are an Eternal Being of Creation.*
>
> — *DIVINITY SPEAKS*

You may be wondering, "That all sounds nice, but *how* do *I* achieve this?" Have you ever heard the phrase *thoughts are energy*? Well, they are! It is widely known that *everything is energy*. What is not commonly known is that this *everything* also includes your thoughts, beliefs, and even how you feel. This is where the ancient wisdom and current scientific evidence meet within the playground of our hearts and the imagination of our minds.

THE BASIC RULE OF ATTRACTION ENERGY

The secret of attraction energy is not really so much of a *secret,* as it is the unrealized potential and wisdom of the ages that is accessible to everyone. It is easily attained when we look beyond what we think we see, and believe we know, as we remember the beauty and truth of who we are as conscious creators.

Modern science shows us there is a physiological and biochemical link between thoughts and emotions. Almost everything we think elicits a feeling or emotion of some kind. The stronger the emotion, the stronger the physiological response your body will experience. Current medical research even shows that the hormones released when we are under prolonged stress can have adverse reactions in our bodies. These reactions may include accelerated aging, illness, and disease. Going beyond these basic facts are the fundamentals of attraction energy and the dividing line between purposefully inspired living and just living.

THE BASIC RULE OF ATTRACTION ENERGY IS EXPLAINED IN NOT JUST HOW YOU THINK, BUT ALSO HOW YOUR THOUGHTS MAKE YOU FEEL. YOUR FEELINGS ARE THE SECRET OF ATTRACTION ENERGY.

How many times have you heard someone remark about how unhappy they are because of events, circumstances, or relationships in their lives? When you have predominantly dreary or negative thoughts focused on what you don't have, what is going wrong, or what is missing in your life or the world, you tend to feel predominately unhappy—you experience a predominantly dismal or unfulfilled life. You suffer from your own sense of expectation and wanting. This is the basic principle of attraction energy in the most *unattractive* form. Please understand, this is in no way passing judgment on anyone. Everyone, including myself, has unhappy thoughts and feelings that are bothersome, unexpected, and seemingly unavoidable. The key here is the word *predominant*. The good news is that attraction energy works *both* ways. We are beings with extraordinary abilities, and we have the potential for quick rebounds based on our thought choices and paying close attention to how we feel.

I know you may be thinking this sounds too simple and too good to be true. I will admit it does sound like a very oversimplified recipe for happiness. But why does it need to be any other way? We always have the power to choose our thoughts, no matter what our situation in life.

CHOOSING YOUR THOUGHTS PURPOSEFULLY, DESPITE HOW CONDITIONS IN YOUR LIFE CURRENTLY APPEAR, IS THE MOST POWERFUL THING YOU CAN DO TO BEGIN THE PROCESS OF POSITIVE TRANSFORMATION.

Many people are not yet ready or open to see the truth and beauty of this simplicity, which has been evading humanity for eons due to familial, cultural, political, and religious fear and guilt-based programming. If you honor this process, the energy of positive transformation will bloom in your life with practice and belief. The following chapters provide more in-depth information to master manifestation through attraction energy. The 12 Keys of Conscious Creation in Part III will show you how.

LOOKING BEYOND

You cannot see that which you do not create. You cannot experience that which you do not believe. You cannot touch what may be there, if it is outside of your awareness.

If you see through the eyes of limitation, your world will be limited.

If you know through the Mind of Expansion, your world will be all you intend it to be and more.

If you wish to experience joy, beauty, love, abundance, peace, and clarity, know this to be true and become your destiny.

Look beyond what you think you see. Look through the eyes of your Soul. The Universe is calling for your awakening.

— *DIVINITY SPEAKS*

4

LOVE, FEAR, AND CONSCIOUS CREATION

> *You become how you feel from one moment to the next.*
>
> — *DIVINITY SPEAKS*

Ancient wisdom and current spiritual teachings share a common belief about how the energy of love and the energy of fear shapes our lives. All thoughts, feelings, and emotions are rooted in two fundamental yet opposing energies. These energies reside within the infinite vibrational spectrum between love and fear. Energetic vibrations can help you harmonize to feel higher or lower on the scale of joy and sorrow. They are all vehicles to transport you from one state of awareness to another.

THE ENERGY OF LOVE

Suppose you think about something that makes you feel happy, peaceful, caring, grateful, abundant, supported, hopeful, connected, and loved. In that case, you will have some kind of feeling or emotion in your body. These types of feelings all vibrate in the higher harmonic, energetic frequencies of what I refer to as *Love Energy*. These types of vibrations generally invoke a peaceful or positive feeling or state of awareness.

THE ENERGY OF FEAR

When you think of something that makes you feel sad, angry, frustrated, worried, hopeless, judgmental, guilty, ashamed, powerless, victimized, or separated, you will also have some kind of feeling or emotion. These types of feelings all vibrate in the lower chaotic, energetic frequencies based on what I call *Fear Energy*. These types of vibrations generally elicit an unsettling or negative feeling or perception.

NEUTRAL ENERGY

Vibrations that reside somewhere in the space in between the energy of love and fear, are what I refer to as *Neutral Energy*. These are the thoughts that don't elicit a feeling or emotion. *Mastering Manifestation* focuses on the vibrations that affect us the most from a *predominant energy* point of view. This book does not spotlight the thoughts that breeze through your mind and don't get tangled in the branches of your awareness. These types of thoughts do not carry the energy and inertia of feeling and emotion—*they just are*. With this said, what I am about to say next is critical in understanding how outcomes in our lives are perceived, magnetized, and ultimately manifested.

THE FREQUENCIES OF LOVE-BASED LIVING AND FEAR-BASED LIVING ARE BOTH EQUALLY POWERFUL IN CONTRIBUTING TO THE OUTCOMES OF YOUR LIFE.

The Universe does not differentiate between positive and negative, good and bad, love, or hate. It says "*YES*" to whatever energetic frequency you *predominately* emit. The more you maintain these *love* frequencies, you tend to attract more positive, desirable, and miraculous outcomes. The more you sustain the *fear* frequencies, you tend to attract more negative, undesirable, and less than optimal outcomes.

> *Many in your society believe creation is a function of your thoughts as in the Law of Attraction. Thoughts and words are a powerful component of your magnetism, for they contain feelings based on either love or fear. The manifestation or outcomes you experience are tied to the magnetic qualities of your predominant energy of love or fear as an individual and a collective.*
>
> — *DIVINITY SPEAKS*

Please understand that I'm not saying loving, caring, and compassionate people will only attract positive things or outcomes in their lives. Although they can, and they do, they can also attract negative things into their lives. Being a loving, caring, and compassionate person doesn't necessarily mean a person wouldn't have fear as his or her predominant energy. There is also karma that we are all here to work out, and karma reaches far beyond the logical mind, and into the realm of spiritual life lessons. We all have a combination of what we perceive as good and bad, as well as ups and downs. It's also not uncommon for the energy of our thoughts, feelings, and emotions to plunge between the highs and lows of daily life. Many, if not all, of our greatest lessons occur as we journey through our deepest pain and our most challenging times. As we move through the discomforts of hardship and suffering, we have the opportunity to evolve and the chance to magnetize new and greater possibilities and potentials.

Notice that I said *opportunity.* Many of us end up repeating the same story with similar adversity with different situations, people, or places, until we finally *get it.* Getting it may also mean that we surrender to our fears, expectations, and control. This is where our lessons can become our greatest teachers. They have the opportunity to guide us towards a more hopeful and optimistic perspective regarding how to think, feel, and believe in a new land of love, peace, possibility, and potential. What I am suggesting in this chapter may be beyond your current belief structure, and this is why I hope you agreed to hold your judgment until the end of this book.

YOU ARE HERE BECAUSE SOMETHING HAS BEEN COMPELLING YOU TO LOOK BEYOND WHAT YOU THINK YOU SEE, OR BELIEVE YOU KNOW.

You were inspired to pick up this book for a reason. Maybe your intuition is awakening, and you are beginning to explore different ideas or different ways of thinking. Perhaps an event has happened that makes you question and challenge your current belief system. Maybe you are tired of doing the same thing over and over again, while always getting the same results.

Whatever brought you here, something deep inside you knows that there is more to creating a happy, fulfilled, healthy, abundant life than simply working hard. Persistence, planning, and work ethics are great qualities to have, but they are not the foundation on which dreams are built.

Your dreams have the opportunity to shape into life fulfilling outcomes as you move from a fear-based belief system into the truth, beauty, and miracles of a love-based belief system. The process of remembering this truth is awakening in me, in you, and in our world at large, through our collective recognition of what has been lying dormant deep inside us. It's time to awaken and remember the *truth of who we are,* as conscious co-creators in the infinite field of imagination and possibility.

> *There is nothing you cannot know, do, create, or be in your world. The key is to know this, and to continue to play as you create. Having fun and living in your joy is instrumental, as is seeing everything through the eyes of love—everything!*
>
> — *DIVINITY SPEAKS*

RESONATING VIBRATIONS AND YOUR SPIRITUAL PATH

Before going into the 12 Keys of Conscious Creation in Part III, I would like to share a little more about resonating vibrations within the energy of love, and the energy of fear. The energy of love is key to harmonizing with the resonant frequencies of your highest potentials, as you will read later. Refer to these when you are not sure which energy you are predominately attracting or emitting. I would also like this to be a reminder. The 12 Keys provide a blueprint for your successful transition from the dream of forgetfulness, to awakening to the truth of who you are as the creator of your dreams. This by no means discounts the importance of a daily spiritual practice that honors whatever spiritual path you are called to follow. This may or may not incorporate religion. The importance of following your spiritual path and being committed and consistent with your spiritual practice, is to keep you present and attuned to the communication within the divinity of your soul. This connection to the Divine Within and *oneness* with everything and everyone, reminds us of our true nature and unites us in a world of seeming separation.

YOUR PREDOMINANT ENERGY IN DAILY LIFE: LOVE OR FEAR

> *When the balance of truth, love over fear, is the predominant nature in your life, dormant forces come alive to aid in the creation of living your life's passions and purpose, as opposed to being caught in the wheel of suffering, boredom, complacency, regret, and un-fulfillment.*
>
> — *DIVINITY SPEAKS*

I have two acronyms that represent the energy of love and fear. They should provide a simple way to help you know where your predominant energy is pointing and a guidepost to where you want to be. Please refer to them often, as you reflect on how you feel or what you think about anything in your life.

In addition to feeling peaceful and positive, I consider the energy of love, as a pure and harmonious vibration. It holds the universal resonance of the Divine. Love energy radiates a consistent and stable frequency, that can bring all other vibrations to a higher and harmonious state.

I think of love energy as PURE, which stands for Positive, Unifying, Regenerating, and Empowering.

As we shift our predominant energy and attention towards living in the PURE energy of love, our lives become harmonious, abundant, free-thinking, and purposefully inspired.

In addition to feeling unsettling or negative, I look at the energy of fear as a chaotic and unstable vibration. It holds the resonance of distortion and disruption. Fear energy can carry distress and disharmony to other frequencies.

I THINK OF FEAR ENERGY AS NEWS, WHICH STANDS FOR NEGATIVE, EXCLUDES, WEAKENS, AND SEPARATES.

As we shift our predominant energy and attention towards NEWS, our lives become discordant, depleted, programmed, and disempowered.

Now, if you are a physicist that has studied the Law of Resonance and the impact of how vibratory energies within the universe affect everything else, I am sure you will agree that my explanations of love and fear energy are highly oversimplified. The important message to understand is that *everything* is affected by the Law of Resonance. This includes your thoughts, words, feelings, emotions, beliefs, intentions, and actions. You always have the ability to choose which stream of energy and vibration to swim in. You also have the ability to *jump* from one stream to another through your vibratory alignment with the energy of love or fear.

EMOTIONS AS TEACHING TOOLS

All emotions are part of the ride in the physical playground called life. They all have the potential to lead to lessons for your evolving Soul.

— *TONITA AWEICA*

Emotions are marvelous things. They are what define us as human. When we experience lower frequency emotions, such as anger, guilt, regret, intolerance, judgment, victimization, hopelessness, greed, or any other disempowering feeling or emotion, we react to life through automatic reflexes. These reflexes are learned behaviors, and habits. All emotions (good and bad) are part of our natural, human responses to situations, conditions, and events, and they should be valued, not dismissed. However, that does not mean that they must be prolonged.

When we reflect on our disempowering emotions, they can be used as teaching tools to help us learn our lessons in life. They can also help guide us to remember our personal truth. They can be used to define *how* we live our lives, recognize what kinds of patterns we tend to get stuck in, and understand what people, circumstances, and things we attract into our lives.

This brings me back to attraction energy. Have you ever been in a situation when you felt depressed, stuck, angry, resentful, powerless, jealous, judgmental, or guilty? Of course you have experienced one or more of these situations. We are all human, and we all experience lower vibrational thoughts, feelings, and emotions from time to time. If we pay attention to our feelings and emotions, we may realize that we sometimes get caught in a loop of repeating the thoughts, behaviors, and actions that lead back to these disempowering ways of feeling. How many times have you started a sentence with the following similar examples?

- I am anxious because …
- I am depressed because …
- I feel hopeless because …
- I can't be happy because …

Please understand that there is no problem with acknowledging how you currently feel. In fact, it is quite healthy. There always needs to be a starting place where you meet the truthful presence of how you feel within yourself. The danger is when your negative or fear-based feelings, emotions, and beliefs turn into a habit. Self-destructive loops of thoughts, feelings, and emotions tend to repeat the same patterns and perpetuate more damaging thoughts, feelings, and emotions. This, in turn, ultimately leads to disempowering, less than optimal outcomes, or *junk* in your life. This is what I call attracting *unattractive* energy.

It is important to note that all thoughts are expressions of our minds, and we are free to choose them. Repeating the same thoughts and then feeling the same emotions, and proceeding with the same actions is how habits are formed. Habits are literally what makes you, you.

The good news is that attraction energy works equally with patterns of higher vibrational thoughts and their corresponding feelings and emotions. Your outcomes become the treasures your heart holds most dear, as you begin to live your life as the *I-am* of positive thoughts, feelings, and actions. There will be more on this later, as well as some exercises to help build the muscle of attraction energy in your life, based on your own personal I-am statements.

ATTRACTION ENERGY—THE MAGNETISM OF THOUGHTS, WORDS, AND EMOTIONS

I assume most people have heard what modern science confirms—everything is energy, and energy vibrates at different frequencies. Frequencies are measurable rates of electrical energy flow between two points. Some frequencies vibrate higher and faster, and some lower and slower, but they all vibrate as they contract and expand. What many people may not think about is what *everything* pertains to. It's easy to imagine that all living things such as people, animals, and plants emit energetic frequencies. It's commonly known that frequencies are emitted from electronic devices such as cell phones, landlines, TV, radio, and computers. We may not know *how* energy transmission works, but we understand that frequencies are a form of energetic information that is sent to a receiver. The Earth, the sun, the moon, and our solar system also vibrate at specific resonant frequencies. What may be less known or thought about is that energetic frequencies are also emitted from inanimate objects such as rocks, minerals, and metal. Even the most mundane things like a paper cup or a thumbtack have a vibration of some kind. Of course, let's not forget about the energetic frequencies of sound, such as your voice and music. Now, take this one step further and apply this law of vibration to intangible or invisible things such as thoughts, words, and emotions.

In our universe of energy and vibration, energetic frequencies are attracted to other energetic frequencies of the same or similar vibrations. When one frequency harmonizes with another, this is called resonance. We have all heard of resonance in music. When music is in harmonic resonance, it vibrates stronger and longer and is more stable, coherent, and organized. In other words, it flows in harmony and balance. Resonance can also apply to the frequencies of your thoughts, words, and emotions. When you get caught in the loop of holding lower energetic frequencies of fear-based thoughts, feelings, and emotions, it's much harder to attract or resonate with the higher energetic frequencies of love-based thoughts, feelings, and emotions. The energy of fear doesn't harmonize and resonate with the energy of love. We are all human transmitters as well as receivers of energy and information. When your thoughts, words, feelings, and emotions predominately vibrate in the energy of fear, you are unable to unlock your fullest potential or happiest life. When your thoughts, words, feelings, and emotions predominately vibrate in the energy of love, your life has the energetic capacity to attract more of what your heart desires. You begin to flow with life instead of against it.

ATTRACTION ENERGY PUT SIMPLY, IS AN INTERACTIVE ACTIVATION OF MAGNETISM BETWEEN WHAT WE THINK, SAY, AND FEEL.

The energy of our thoughts activates our feelings, which are like magnets that pull the resonating frequencies to us. Information is communicated within these electromagnetic energy fields between thoughts and feelings, which attract the outcomes of infinite possibilities. You have heard it said before, "What you send out, you get back in return." This is a straightforward explanation of karma, and is also a fundamental premise of attraction energy.

IMAGINATION CREATION

As you become the presence of your own power and remember your connection to the Divine through the practice of imagination creation, your reality is shaped to the outcome of what you desire. This Law of Manifestation works individually as well as collectively. For an individual, in reality, is also the collective.

— *DIVINITY SPEAKS*

In 1944, one of my favorite mystics and revered spiritual leaders of his time, Neville Goddard, wrote a book titled *Feeling Is the Secret*. He believed that consciousness is the cause, as well as the substance of the world. Through our power to imagine and feel, along with our freedom to choose our thoughts and ideas, we have control over creating our lives. This is another way of saying that different frequencies of energy are attracted into our lives by how we imagine, feel, and, therefore, create. I call this *imagination creation.* All dreams are born within our inspired imagination.

OUR FEELINGS AND EMOTIONS ATTRACT THE ENERGETIC FREQUENCIES OF LOVE OR FEAR, DEPENDING ON HOW WE FEEL IN EVERY MOMENT.

When we become conscious of *fear-based,* lower, disempowering emotions and replace them with *love-based,* higher, empowering emotions, our lives *attract* the *possibilities* and *dreams* of our greatest desires. When we begin living in this love-based attraction reality, there is no limit as to what our imagination has, until now, only been able to wish for.

We begin to live our lives with renewed purpose and abundance. Instead of feeling like life is one big struggle to swim upstream, life begins to flow easily and effortlessly. Things, circumstances, and people come into your life that support you and add value to your goals and dreams. And as if that is not enough, we also have the ability to be healthier and more vital. We even have the potential to heal ourselves in a myriad of ways through the successful application of attraction energy.

In the stillness of your mind is a connection to The Universe. It is important to remember that this Universe is not outside of you. Accessing this connection is as simple as remembering that your outside world is only a reflection of what you create on the inside. Knowing that there is no separation

is the key to this understanding and the catalyst for unlimited creation. Any fear and self-doubt block the gateway to this timeless place of eternal consciousness. For the fear that is inside of you is created into a multitude of obstacles in the reflection of your reality. The key to removing these obstacles is removing the fear. The key to removing the fear is to know that fear is only of your own creation. You become the master of your own creation by remembering the truth of who you are.

— *DIVINITY SPEAKS*

NOT JUST POSITIVE THINKING

Attraction energy is *not* just the power of positive thinking. If it were, then it would be more successful for more people. Being positive and thinking positive thoughts are certainly vital ingredients in the recipe for a happy, fulfilled life. Other ingredients are needed to master manifestation and make the recipe complete. Let's take a look!

INGREDIENTS FOR ATTRACTION ENERGY

- The power of inspired imagination
- The power of positive feeling
- The power of positive thinking
- The power of words
- The power of belief

- The power of heartfelt intention

When used consistently, while applying the 12 Keys of Conscious Creation, you have a recipe that will magnetize your highest potentials and your heartfelt dreams as:

- Inspired actions
- Opportunities
- Events
- Things
- People
- Abundance
- Wealth
- Health
- And so much more!

It is important to note that it's not only your actions that lead you to the life of your dreams; it is your imagination, your thinking, your feelings, your beliefs, and your words that usher you towards infinite possibilities and outcomes of imagination creation.

ABOUT REALITY CREATION

So much has been said about creating your reality. As the human mind searches for answers to explain the Universal Truths of creation, you reach for words to describe concepts that are only really understood at the level of the knowing Soul.

You reach for complex answers to the simplest of questions. One of which is a basic misunderstanding of reality creation. It is not possible to create a "new" reality when the infinite presence of Source has always been and always will be. What this means is that within the presence of each moment you call time, exists every situation, every outcome, every opportunity, event, function, and life path.

At the level of the thinking mind, you language that creating your reality is a function of what you do or how you think as in the Law of Attraction. While this is partially true, the vital key to this law is how you individually, as well as collectively, vibrate and then radiate via your joys as well as your fears.

Reality creation is, in actuality, reality attraction. You attract the reality that most resonates with your current vibration. You experience the world, which you attract into your individual and collective reality, both knowingly and unknowingly. This will not be the same individual or collective reality for someone else.

Following your heart for the purpose of bringing more love and joy to yourself will ultimately bring you closer to knowing your destiny and purpose on this Earth. See and radiate the beauty of the world, be open to opportunities, maintain or restore relationships that are meant to serve you, and heal yourself in ways you can only imagine, while ultimately living the life of your dreams.

— *DIVINITY SPEAKS*

PART III

THE 12 KEYS OF CONSCIOUS CREATION

"You are the Light in which you shine. You are the Beauty in which you see. You are the Truth in which you know. You are the Love in which you feel. You are the Source of all you create. Take these Keys to unlock the inner chambers of Infinite Possibility and set the barriers of fear and illusion free."

— *DIVINITY SPEAKS*

ABOUT THE KEYS

All 12 Keys of Conscious Creation in this book are designed to open your understanding of just how vital it is to be aware of your predominant energy, in order to be in alignment with your most creative life and inspired dreams. Most in the Western culture, and throughout the world, are not taught from childhood to understand the creative power held within the energy of thoughts, words, *and* feelings. They have also not learned how vital all three of these combined factors are in contributing to the conscious creation of our individual, as well as our collective realities.

The 12 Keys are a blueprint to consciously become the master of your own manifestation, versus being the victim of circumstance. Think of it as creatively flowing within your destiny, versus stagnating within your fate. If we had a choice (and we all do), I think most of us would pick creation over stagnation. In actuality, we all master manifestation every single day of our lives. The outcomes we experience through our mastery are primarily based on the predominant energy of our thoughts, feelings, *and* emotions. However, most people do not know the alchemizing power they hold within themselves to consciously and powerfully magnetize and create the life of their dreams through the secret of attraction energy.

It is important to note that the 12 Keys are a continual and dynamic process. The virtues of life are to be included every step of the way as your guiding light toward purpose and meaning. Virtues are not only living by moral excellence and ethical principles, they are the essence of our character and an expression of our souls. When we bring them into our everyday awareness, they have an amazing ability to remind us of our inherent, although often overlooked, capacity to be our own examples of living life with a commitment to love and devotion to our highest calling and purpose.

Virtues such as kindness, gratitude, forgiveness, honesty, and tolerance are the foundation upon which the 12 Keys are built. These Keys could not exist without them. Just as you cannot build a physical bridge without the proper physical materials, the 12 Keys rely on the nonphysical materials of what virtues represent in order to be realized. Of course, there are many more virtues than what I stated above. I am not listing them all in this book, as there are more than one hundred of them and probably a lot more.

The following are some additional examples of virtues. I encourage you to read each one as you become present with the meaning of the word. Allow your body to feel the energy that each virtue represents. This can also be incorporated into a powerful meditation, which can bring a renewed sense of purpose and passion for life. Virtues help awaken and deepen your connection within yourself, others, and the Divine. Reflect upon the virtues often as you read, and then reread, through the 12 Keys, and then apply them to your life. Don't hesitate to learn more about the other virtues that are not listed in this book.

EXAMPLES OF VIRTUES

- Kindness
- Gratitude
- Patience
- Caring
- Compassion
- Forgiveness
- Peace
- Honesty
- Joyfulness
- Acceptance
- Service
- Reverence
- Tolerance
- Unity
- Faith
- Grace
- Humility
- Love
- Confidence
- Courage

5

KEY 1

IMAGINATION IS CREATION

You are the source of your dreams and the truth of your imagination.

— *DIVINITY SPEAKS*

Throughout the ages, science and spirituality share a common thread within the ever-flowing tapestry of the Universe. That thread is imagination. From spiritual teachers to scientists, many great minds write about the magnetic power and influence of imagination being more important than intellect in attracting and creating outcomes in our lives. In a universe that abides by attraction energy, our human imagination is a critical Key for magnetizing our dreams into reality.

Let me just point out before going any further about the difference between thinking and dreaming. They are both essential ingredients to attract outcomes in our lives. One can have thought without imagination, but imagination is dependent on a thought to spark its creative potential.

We have thoughts all day long. Some are charged with energy and emotion, some are not. Most thoughts skip through our minds as a light breeze flows through the branches of a tree. We may or may not even notice them. Some thoughts get tangled in the branches of our awareness and we either set them free or allow them to accumulate. The thoughts that collect are the ones that we begin focusing on. They become more predominant or repeated in our minds. Still, they may or may not carry the energy of emotion.

As our thoughts continue to collect, we begin to put meaning to them. They eventually build into various systems within us. Beliefs, goals, plans, wants, needs, and intentions are all interconnected within the energy of our thoughts. When kept in the darkness of our inattention, they are merely the seeds of unplanted possibilities and potentials. As more attention is placed on our thoughts, they begin to acquire energy and inertia to sprout and grow. They require the light of our awareness to be kept alive and continue to thrive. But what provides the fuel to feed their hungry nature? That is where the power of your imagination steps in and says, "Hello. I'm here!"

FEELING THE DREAM FULFULLED

As important as it is to focus your attention on what you want to generate in your life, it is vital to imagine, as well as feel, what you want to have, do, be, and create. This does not mean just wish or think. It means to truly *dream* and then *feel* the dream as if it has already happened. Your inspired imagination deeply ties into attraction energy, because imagination, when ignited by your deepest desires, is magnetized with high-frequency thoughts *and* feelings. This in turn, helps attract the outcomes of your dreams. Therefore, it is vital to envision as well as *feel* the dream fulfilled, and not how your current circumstances appear to be.

YOU EXPERIENCE AND BECOME WHAT YOU IMAGINE THROUGH ATTRACTION ENERGY. YOU DO THIS BY FEELING THE DESIRED OUTCOME AS IF IT HAS ALREADY OCCURRED.

The best thing about this is that scientific research now shows that the subconscious mind cannot tell the difference between imagination and reality. As you *imagine* and then *feel* a life of already fulfilled dreams, supportive relationships, purpose, prosperity, and abundant health, the energy from your imagination, and the power of your subconscious mind work together to support and create the life of your dreams through the inspiration of your imagination.

You will achieve your greatest satisfaction and see your most desired outcomes in life when your inspired imagination leads the way.

— *DIVINITY SPEAKS*

EXERCISE 1

IDENTIFY YOUR DREAMS

This is an opportunity for you to become present with your hopes and dreams. Take a blank journal or notebook, or open your computer and write or type them all down. Don't limit yourself! Touch base with your most delicious and desirable dreams from various stages of your life. You may not want or feel attracted to some of these anymore, and that's okay. Even if you think your wants, wishes, hopes, dreams, and desires are silly, unrealistic, or no longer possible for various reasons, this Key is *vital* in the process of beginning to reawaken your imagination and reestablish a heart-mind/higher-self connection. It is within this playground that all inspired creation happens through heart-felt imagination.

Please take a fair amount of quality time with this exercise before going on to the next one. After writing a page, or several pages, of what you long to do, have, or become, you will start to recognize which of these things are less than meaningful hopes, or expired or no longer important dreams, and which ones are the current dreams that your soul is seeking. Ask your heart what it has to say about the dreams you have identified, and write it all down. Hold nothing back, and keep it truthful. As long as you are writing from a place of love and honesty, there are no wrong answers. You can keep an open dialogue with your higher self through the channel of your heart. Keep this exercise fun! The second you begin to doubt yourself or your ability to actualize the dreams you identified from your higher self, then the energy of fear and doubt will begin to prevail. This type of energy interrupts and prolongs the process of completion. Keep your journal to refer to as you continue with your process. I suggest you refer to it daily or, better yet, refer to it several times a day, so that it may help stimulate your subconscious mind to access and accept your dreams. For the dreams you genuinely wish to manifest, it is vitally important to incorporate the energy of imagination and gratitude, as you see and feel the dream realized. (See the next exercise.) You can revise your dreams, add to your dreams, or even delete your dreams anytime you like. Yes, there is nothing wrong with hitting the delete button and starting over. This is a sacred journey through your imagination, and it is for your eyes only.

> *Look beyond what you think you see. Your world is what you imagine it to be*
>
> — *DIVINITY SPEAKS*

Exercise 2
JOURNEY INTO YOUR IMAGINATION AND FEEL YOUR DREAM FULFILLED

Before you begin your journey to your imagination, you will first need to define your desires. What do you really want to have, do, be, create, or achieve? This can be big or small, but always make sure that it is based on the energy of love and not fear. For example, your own modification of this exercise should be used for the fulfillment of your dreams and the betterment of others. The exercise should not be used to bring anything other than positive outcomes in all situations. The energy of consciousness is magnetic. If your intentions are not pure and are based on the energy of fear or negativity, you are attracting the energy you emit back to yourself based on the strength of your desires.

Personally, my best time to create is when my body is completely relaxed, and my mind is peaceful. Relaxation does not always mean sitting or lying down. Some of my most profound and powerful meditations on what I wish to create have been riding as a passenger on my husband's motorcycle. In this place of complete and utter surrender of all things physical, my mind is free to take a break and wander within the playground of my imagination. The outlines of my desires become fully colored with the details of completing my dream come true as I let go and journey within.

As I begin to imagine what I wish to do, be, have, or create, I see and feel the completion of the dream. The details become alive in my mind's eye as I marry the feeling of fulfillment with various items that would occur in the intended outcome. This may include sounds, smells, surroundings, objects, and other people. As my imagination continues to build, I think about what I am seeing, doing, hearing, saying, and touching. I do not imagine the event as an observer; I imagine it as if I am participating in the outcome of my dream fulfilled and not standing back or looking on. I actually feel myself there, and I feel as well as see the object of my desire complete in my mind's eye. I also pay attention to my sense of gratitude, and I anchor that feeling by silently repeating, "thank you." I believe bringing the energy of gratitude into the equation is a powerful force.

Now, please don't think you need to start riding a motorcycle. This is just one example of how I relax and bask in the waves of attraction energy. I have many other avenues that help bring me to a deep and timeless awareness within my imagination, and so do you. The key is to discover what they are and then modify this example exercise to fit your own personal path of dream development.

I would be remiss if I didn't mention the value of sitting or lying down in a quiet meditative state to begin your journey into your imagination. When you are in a relaxed and peaceful state, your subconscious is very receptive, and you can still direct your thoughts. There are few nights when I do not venture into my imagination before going to sleep, as I continue to feel my dream fulfilled. This provides a peaceful beginning for my sleep state and helps anchor my dream within my subconscious. However, I will admit that when I do this, I tend to not get very far in my imagination before I fall asleep. I think it is because feeling the dream fulfilled is such a peaceful, rewarding thing to focus on, that it acts like a calming agent. Sometimes when I wake at night and cannot go back to sleep, imagining a dream fulfilled is the best sleeping pill I could possibly take!

THE LAW OF IMAGINATION CREATION

Set aside your to-do list. Create an experience list. Write down some things you wish to experience in your career. Write down some things you wish to experience in your personal life. Write down some things you wish to experience in your relationships. Write down some things you wish to experience in your spirituality. Remember the things you write are merely the expressions of how you want to feel, as you imagine them into existence. Realize these things are what you long to experience, not achieve. For when something is achieved, the experience is over in your reality. You then move to the next dream.

If you live in the to-do's of life, the joy is diminished as one thing is crossed off the list, and another thing is entered. The joy of the journey is how you feel when you are in the creation phase of your imagination. If you strive only for the end goal of the creation phase, you miss the beauty and joy of the journey, and then the moment feels empty once it appears in your reality.

Moments are fleeting in your perception of time and existence. Moments are not things to be realized as an end result of a goal. They represent the culmination of the journey toward your dream. You have many journeys and many dreams to realize and experience. Do not make your life about achieving any of them. Make your life about dreaming for them and knowing that dreaming is where your power lies to manifesting your destiny.

A to-do list holds you in bondage and creates anxiety when you feel you are not getting enough done. Realize that your most fulfilled life is not about getting things done. It's about reaching for how it makes you feel during the creation phase of the dream. The manifestation of the dream is secondary to the lessons of your achievements, and it is in knowing your capabilities of bringing your desires into existence. Realize that they all exist already. It's just a matter of opening up to the correct vision and then seeing, perceiving, and feeling yourself in that moment of time.

It is impossible for this to fail as per the Law of Imagination Creation. You are a master of Imagination Creation, which is the art of allowing yourself to not only dream, but also feel the thrill of your own creative journey as it springs into life.

— *DIVINITY SPEAKS*

6

KEY 2

BE PRESENT NOW

> *The road of your destiny is paved by the joy of your now. Be present with your highest desires, and see your dreams manifest into the glorious creations of your Soul. Light, Love, and Beauty will illuminate the way to the path of your purpose and the actualization of your dreams.*
>
> — *DIVINITY SPEAKS*

Much has been written about the Law of Attraction and the power of being in the present moment, and for good reason! This Key is paramount to unlocking the door of conscious creation and attracting your destiny from the field of infinite possibilities. In reality, all outcomes are available as they magnetize to you, from your predominant energy of thoughts, feelings, and emotions. This is why it is vital to become aware of your predominant energy and shift it as necessary. For it is only within the moments of *now* in which our fate or destiny is attracted to us from the infinite field of possibility and potential.

As mentioned earlier, the energy of love is pivotal to help magnetize the frequencies of your highest potentials. Love is the source that lights the way. Your imagination is the vehicle that takes you to your inspired destiny. Being truly present unites you with the neutral space within the genesis of creation. Being more present and peaceful with *all moments of now* is the Key to unlocking the outcomes you most desire in life. This is really just another way to explain that you attract how you predominantly think, feel, speak, and act.

When we live our lives in perpetual fear, whether it is worry, hopelessness, and stress about the future, or sorrow, anger, and remorse about the past, the door to our most joyful and inspired destiny remains not only closed, but locked. Many people do not realize that each of us holds our own key to unlock destiny's door. We all have the opportunity to open the door once we unlock it and then walk into the infinite field of our possibilities and highest potentials. The greatest version of the life you have always dreamed of having, doing, or becoming is within this field. You have the power to magnetize and live the life you dream of through this key.

YOU HOLD THE KEY TO UNLOCK AND MANIFEST YOUR MOST DESIRED POTENTIALS THROUGH YOUR PRESENT MOMENTS OF NOW, AND NOW, AND NOW.

As a society, we are more than ever becoming disengaged and disconnected from moments of now. How many times today have you worried about something or someone? How many times today have you felt remorse or sadness about something that happened in the past? How many times today have you worried or stressed about the future? All of these fear-based thoughts and feelings bring you away from the destiny your soul longs for you to experience.

Even though I would like to, I am not going to tell you to stop worrying altogether. Part of our human experience is to do just that—to experience. From experience, we have the opportunity to learn and grow. What I am suggesting is to pay attention to how many times a day you are pulled from being in the present moment with thoughts or feelings of worry, stress, anxiety, hopelessness, anger, judgment, and so on, whether it is about you, someone else, or conditions in the world.

As a specific example, how many times have you picked up your cell phone today to look at an email, respond to a text, scroll through or post on social media, look at the weather, check the news or stock market, see what your cryptocurrency is up to, or play a game? We will address this in a later Key, but please begin to think about it now. While technology can educate and unite, it can also perpetuate the fear-based programming and greatly distract us from simply being present within the precious moments of now.

Exercise 3
BE PRESENT NOW MEDITATION

This is one of my favorite meditations for connecting with the present moment. The wonderful thing about this exercise is that it can be done during various times and in various places and not just sitting in one place. I do caution you that if you need to focus on a matter of the physical, such as driving, then reserve this meditation for another time when you are able to just *be* in the moment.

I like to do this as a type of mindful meditation while walking on the beach, hiking in the woods, riding on the back of my husband's motorcycle, or anytime I can shift my awareness from outward appearances and become present within. In this inward-focused attention, I try to imagine myself becoming one with the thing or feeling I am focusing on. You may choose to focus on something physical like a candle flame or a beautiful tree. I suggest if you focus on something physical that you make sure it represents something spiritual, meaningful, uplifting, or beautiful to you. Focusing on a cement wall, for example, may not give you the initial feeling of reverence, connection, depth, or wonder you will need to *listen within*. You may also choose to focus on something nonphysical, like a feeling such as gratitude or caring. For example, I will use a walking meditation, as my heart expands into not just seeing, but also feeling the beauty of nature around me and within me.

Before I start my walk, I make sure my cell phone ringer is turned off, to keep from diverting my attention away from the moment. As I begin walking, I become present and aware of my surroundings. I breathe in the feelings of peace and gratitude as a signal for my mind to let go, and my heart to lead. In this state of focused awareness, my attention will begin to shift to each tree I pass. My only thoughts are on the trees, as I become immersed in their majestic beauty and elegance. I notice how their branches harmoniously sway with the whispers of the passing breezes. I notice their colors, their vibrancy, and their aliveness. I feel their strong inner resolve, their deep-rooted ties to Mother Earth, and their unified connection to the wholeness of the Universe.

Inwardly, I open up to the beauty, truth, and oneness I share with all of nature. If I begin to think about something else, I simply remind myself to focus on the trees, and their majestic elegance as they stand tall and true, and I focus on all the secrets and ancient wisdom they hold. My thoughts become stilled as I begin to look beyond what I think I see, and begin to perceive through the inner-vision of my heart. In this state of awareness, I feel the same Divine Presence within the tree as the Divine Presence within me. My heart remains open and connected to this loving presence of the Divine, as my consciousness is immersed in the beauty of nature and the blissful oneness within all things.

Although it is entirely within your reach, I do not expect you to feel this level of love and connection with the trees or with nature on your first walking meditation. You will be developing a new or expanded sense of perception. As with learning anything new, you shouldn't expect perfection the first time you try it. If you need to start by *imagining* the loving Presence within the trees and within you, then that's okay. The door to inward exploration is often opened by the imagination, as it takes you on a journey of self-discovery within. If you don't try, then you will never know.

As my walking meditation continues, my thoughts become dormant while my heart unites within this Presence. My body recognizes the familiarity of the oneness within all things. I feel my breath become one with the breath with the Universe. I feel the beauty of this truth coursing throughout my entire body. It fills me with a deep sense of calmness, inner peace, and connection. With practice, this type of mindful meditation can be done anytime and anywhere. It can take seconds to minutes or even longer. The point is to start with your imagination as the gateway, and then allow yourself to unite with the peaceful and harmonious loving presence of oneness within the Divine Universe.

THE POWER OF PEACE

> *The more peaceful you become, the more powerful you are.*
>
> — *DIVINITY SPEAKS*

Uniting with the beauty and radiance of our inner peace is a foundation that all other Keys are built upon. The presence of the moment, united with our inner peace, effortlessly flows within the field of dreams as it dances in unison with the inspired imagination. The inward presence of peace, harmony, and grace supercharges the magnet of your imagination and amplifies the energy of your highest emotions. This could have also been listed as Key 1, but these Keys are not linear, and there really is no order for the dynamic nature of accessing Infinite Intelligence and attracting the energy of your desired reality. Up and down, first and last, beginning and ending are all functions of the human mind. The energy of one heart, one mind, one soul, holds and unifies the infinite, eternal, ever-present, and all-knowing, Peace within all things. If you really desire to attract and create the life of your dreams, this Key should be infused within you as a mantra to be continuously remembered and accessed throughout your journey and your life.

WHAT IS PEACE?

Before we go any further, I would like to ask you two questions: What does peace mean to you? What does it feel like?

Peace is a subjective word that will mean different things to different people, and feel different ways. Have you ever stopped to wonder what it really means to you or how you actually *feel* when you are peaceful? To some, it may mean a sense of security or feeling calm. To others, it may mean feeling happy, loved, or fulfilled. On a broader scale, peace represents ending war or hostility between nations, groups, and individuals. I think most would agree that being in a peaceful state means there are no conflicting emotions while there is a sense of harmony and acceptance within oneself.

Whatever manner you personally describe or feel peace, it is something that we all have the ability to tune in to. What many may not know is that there is a difference between the emotional/physical aspect of peace, and connecting with your true inner peace.

WHAT IS THE DIFFERENCE BETWEEN PEACE AND INNER PEACE?

Peace is something we have the ability to experience and often yearn to find. It is, however, conditional in relation to what is going on around us. How we feel can significantly change during times of inner turmoil and external conflict. Things such as anger, fear, greed, hostility, judgment, violence, and attachments can steal our peace. This, in turn, may impact how we view and react to our own personal position and feelings of peace, when less-than-peaceful circumstances are occurring in our world, our communities, and even our homes. As an example, I am in the final editing phase of this book amid the COVID-19 pandemic. There are too many examples of conflict, dissension, separation, and hostility to mention. While the world is at war with an unseen invader, as well as each other's opinions and judgments, peace is not something that is widely recognized. Yet, even amid the upheaval of the world, more and more people are learning how to connect with their inner peace. They are uniting with the truth and oneness that transcends all fear-based thoughts, feelings, and emotions. Inner peace is experiencing a sense of oneness and spiritual bliss.

Inner peace is deeply embedded into the essence of who we are as spiritual beings within the harmony of the Divine Universe. It rides on every breath we take, yet is only truly experienced when we drop attachment to, and expectation of, achieving a specific outcome and surrender the ego. It's not that we don't wish for a peaceful world, we simply remember that *we* are the peace we are seeking. It extends beyond the perceptions of worldly ties and appearances.

INNER PEACE IS NOT SOMETHING YOU NEED TO FIND, IT IS SOMETHING YOU ARE.

When you need to find something, it implies that you don't already have it. Inner peace is not dependent on anything apparently external from yourself, so therefore, it can never be truly lost. It can, however, be hidden from your current state of awareness. This is true especially when outside influences such as events or other people can shift your attention from your natural state of inner peace to worry, stress, fear, or anxiety.

Peace is a frequency or an energetic vibration of the Divine. It may appear not to be available when you are focused or tuned in to lower frequencies of energy such as fear, anger, or hopelessness. It is, however, always available if you so choose to change your channel or state of mind from fear-based thoughts and feelings, to love-based thoughts and feelings.

UNITING WITH YOUR INNER PEACE

Uniting with your inner peace can often feel elusive. When you perceive life through the lens of the conditioned mind, it is rare to experience a true sense of inner peace. Our minds often put limitation and expectation on how we *should* feel or what we *should* experience, when we try to slow down or connect through meditation.

As we go about our daily lives, we often operate from our lower chakras (root to solar plexus). Rushing against the clock to cram everything we need to accomplish in a 24-hour day, is a sure fire plan to keep you disconnected and distracted. While important to our human existence, our lower chakras keep us embedded and focused on the physical/material aspects of life and things we need to do just to survive.

Connecting with your inner peace begins when you become present with your heart or what is also known as the fourth chakra. It opens you to a deeper communion within yourself as well as the Universe. As the mind learns to be in communion (sacred conversation) with the heart, we experience our first sense of spiritual awakening by becoming present with our true inner nature (the Divine within).

There is a remembrance deep within each of us, that knows the truth of who we are as love, light, peace, and infinite wisdom. We are each here to experience different things in this life and learn various lessons. Many of us have forgotten the deep truth of our peaceful origins due to karmic reasons, conditioning, beliefs, events, habits, patterns, and circumstances.

INNER PEACE IS EXPERIENCED BY:

- Reestablishing an open and intimate relationship between you, your higher self, and the Divine Universe, despite outer circumstances or appearances. It is the remembrance and truth of who you are!

- Becoming present with the Prana (life-force energy within you). Prana is sometimes referred to as breath, or the breath of life, and may be accessed by mindful/heartful breathing, meditation, and mantra.

- Letting go and surrendering to attachments of outcomes, desires, and the appearance of the physical world and its perceived chaotic state.

- Shifting your awareness or state of consciousness from disharmonious or chaotic affairs of the physical world, including other people, circumstances, and events, to the Divine harmony within.

- Practicing detached compassion, forgiveness, and non-judgment of self and others. Forgiveness is key to opening the heart and experiencing the vibration of peace within.

INNER PEACE IS NOT:

- Anything you do or have in the physical world, or anything perceived to be outside of yourself. It is not about money, jobs, relationships, things, other people, circumstances, or events. While these things may provide a sense of security, happiness, relief, or even peace, this is not true inner peace.

- Focusing on what is going wrong or what you are worried about. This will attract the exact opposite results of the state you desire. Due to the bombardment of negative or chaotic influences in our lives, this is not always easy to remember or achieve.

- Memories of the past or even dreams of the future.

CONNECTING WITH YOUR INNER PEACE

Establishing a relationship between the physical you, your higher self, and the Divine Universe can be accomplished in various ways. A well-known example of connecting with inner peace is by becoming present through the practice of prayer, or meditation and mantra. When I talk about connecting to your inner peace through prayer, this does not mean to ask for something to change or asking for something you want or need in your physical world. Inner peace is not reached through anything outside of yourself. Prayer, meditation, and mantra are vehicles to help you achieve a state of awareness to your connection with Divinity. This is achieved as you feel the presence of the Divine within, and you connect to your true inner bliss.

INNER PEACE IS YOUR TRUE NATURE AND STATE OF BEING

Becoming present with the *now* of life is crucial. True inner peace is experienced within the present moment, which becomes your sacred communication/communion with the Divine.

Your inspired actions, thoughts, feelings, or getting lost in the moment can help connect you to your inner peace. Some examples may be listening to music, walking in nature, playing an instrument, dancing, writing, painting, practicing yoga and doing other forms of exercise. There have been many times I've become lost in the moment as I rocked my children and grandchildren as babies. It's not what you do, it's how you *feel* as you transcend beyond anything other than being immersed in the present moment.

Higher vibrations such as unconditional love, genuine gratitude, joy, beauty, deep appreciation, and caring can help bring you to a state of inner peace once you learn how to heartfully focus on those states of awareness. Mantra is also a wonderful and very effective method to use as a gateway to that blissful state of being.

Some peaceful or joyful memories of the past or dreams of the future may bring you a feeling of peace. This can be a powerful tool during meditation to use as a gateway to join you with your true inner peace. It is important to remember that these memories or dreams are merely vehicles. While they may provide joy or feelings of peacefulness, they are not your true inner peace.

Connecting with your inner peace is the best way to reconnect with your purpose in life. It speaks directly to your heart from the sacred language of the Divine. Life lessons are learned through the lens of love, acceptance, compassion, and forgiveness. This ultimately opens the door to new, exciting opportunities to expand your potential and live life with a renewed sense of clarity and direction.

There are thousands and probably millions of ways people become present with the deep and still waters of the peace within. The purpose of this book is not to provide all of those ways. There are countless books and resources on meditation and how to become present within yourself. For purposes of example only, I have included some types of meditation that are effective for me. That is not to say that this will be as effective for you. Feel free to use my examples, and then structure them into something that resonates for you.

Meditation is a very personal journey through timeless inward reflection. As your practice deepens, the sense of self, or I, dissolves as you begin to merge into the remembrance of the oneness you share with all of reality. With patience and practice, it can lead to profound insights, revelations, transformation, and self-discovery. It can be used as a vehicle to help you awaken to your highest truth, inner peace, spiritual bliss, and connection with whatever the Divine means to you. As you remember your true nature, your life becomes a living prayer.

Now, don't worry if all of the above sounds a bit far-fetched or unattainable. There is no race and no rule that says you must, you should, or you will become completely absorbed and transformed through meditation. *Please* take the stress, worry, or expectation entirely out of the equation. Just begin, and see what happens. Play with different styles of meditation. Find what works for you. If you need some additional assistance, there are countless teachers, such as myself, who teach different meditation techniques to help you find your own path to peacefulness.

On a final note, there are plenty of documented scientific studies on the benefits of meditation. Some of these studies have shown how meditation helps to decrease stress and stress-induced illness. Medical research also reveals how regular meditation has an amazing variety of other benefits, such as brain preservation and the ability to combat and transform depression, anxiety, and pain. Other known benefits are improved sleep, concentration, learning, and memory. It is impossible to mention all of the wonderful benefits and effects of meditation. If you are interested, I would encourage you to do your own research.

HEARTFUL BREATHING

One type of meditation I often recommend is something that even the most novice meditator can easily incorporate into his or her daily life. Mindful, heartful breathing is one of the most amazing, rejuvenating, energizing, and energy-shifting things you can do to change how you think and feel, and what you ultimately attract. Just the act of heartful breathing is a meditation in itself. The best thing is that it can be done anywhere, and it only has to take a moment once you get the hang of it.

The study of heart intelligence is an emerging science that proves our hearts have an intelligence that is independent of the brain. The heart not only senses and feels from an intuitive standpoint, but communicates directly with the brain to signal how we think and how our bodies function. When our brain waves harmonize with our heart waves, the more clear, balanced, and peaceful we become and the more effective we are in managing the challenges of life.

As we begin to replace feelings of stress (fear-based energy) with feelings of peace (love-based energy), our imagination opens as the restrictions of stress transform into possibilities that were not previously seen, felt, or imagined. It is as if a whole new world appears that was right before your eyes, but you were blinded by the darkness of stress and limitation.

As one begins to learn and practice heartful breathing regularly, and incorporates it into everyday life, a foundation is set that supports the other Keys. The Keys begin to make sense from a heart and soul level, versus an intellectual level. The work does not seem to be work, as inner transformation is experienced, and outcomes are seen, felt, and, more importantly, known. This explanation is my personal experience of heart intelligence on a spiritual level. You can learn more about the study of heart intelligence online. This is something I highly recommend.

Exercise 4
HEARTFUL BREATHING MEDITATION

Heartful breathing is a heart-centered breathing meditation. It does not have to be long, and it can be done anywhere, at any time, with your eyes open or closed. Any low vibrational, disempowering thoughts, feelings, and emotions can be transformed into higher vibrational empowering energy in an instant. For deeper relaxation, close your eyes when you are in a place that does not require your attention. Closing your eyes helps filter out visual distractions as you focus your attention inward.

- Begin by placing a hand (or both hands) over your heart. This is a physical reminder that you are connecting with your heart space and inner peace.

- Take a long deep breath in through your nose as you set your intention to feel peaceful within.

- Feel the air enter slowly and evenly.

- Gently and deeply fill your lungs.

- Allow your abdomen to expand with each breath.

- Imagine you are breathing in peace, love, calmness, and clarity deep into your heart.

- Imagine and *feel* your breath funneling in through your heart and infusing your entire body with the energy of peace. This may take some practice, but once you get it, you will never forget it.

- After practicing how that feels for a few breaths or a few minutes (whatever you have time for), imagine you are exhaling everything that does not serve you—worries, stress, fear, and so on. *Feel* those disempowering energies, thoughts, and things gently releasing from your mind and body.

- As you continue with this process you begin to feel more room for the expansion of love, peace, calmness, and clarity with each inhalation.

- Continue to breathe in the energy of peace through your heart, as it infuses your body and helps you feel lighter and calmer with each passing breath. Get creative with your imagination. You may want to visualize and feel a soft, warm, soothing light entering your heart area as you breathe in, or imagine a sparkling, loving radiance streaming through you from the Divine. Continue to release the energies that no longer serve you.

One breath is all you need to upgrade your current state and start feeling better. This is helpful if you don't have the time or are not in a place that will permit you to continue for a more extended period. If you continue to do this heartful breathing for a longer period of time and incorporate it into your everyday life, it will aid in transitioning the predominant lower energetic frequencies you may be experiencing to a higher nature. This not only transforms the moment, but it provides the foundational structure to enhance and support the other Keys. When doing this meditation, I like to think about, and then feel, other high vibrations such as love, compassion, gratitude, caring, and joy. If you include this step, it is a wonderful expansion of your experience into the beauty, unity, and oneness within the present moment and your intimate connection to Source.

Looking within, what surrounds you is inside you. Go deeper into yourself to access the Truth. Inside is what contains the visions of your world and the illuminations of the knowing Soul. By being in a peaceful state, you can access this abundance. Breathe this in with your heart, as it becomes your today. Today is the now for the birth of your tomorrow, and the catalyst of all creation. As this moment inspires beauty and love, you will continue to know, grow, open, and transform yourself into the world your heart most desires and your Soul rejoices for.

— *DIVINITY SPEAKS*

7

KEY 3

RECOGNIZE YOUR PATTERNS

> *Do not look for the path to appear. It appears the moment you know it into creation.*
>
> — *DIVINITY SPEAKS*

The next Key to attract and create a more joyful, abundant, fulfilled, vibrant, purposeful, and even healthier life, is to recognize your own personal patterns of disempowering and self-repeating thoughts, emotions, and actions. We all have them. If you don't know what they are right away, just be patient.

Your personal patterns, which are a big part of your personality, will show themselves to you as you begin to pay attention to how you predominately feel. This is very important in identifying whether it is your conditioned mind or your unconditioned heart that rules your personal story of life.

Living in your truth means living a life led by your heart. When the conditioned mind dominates your heart, truth and purpose take a back seat to your dreams and fullest potential. If the mind rules, there is much you can do to nurture a true partnership and communication between heartful and mindful living, as you practice, and then master the Keys going forward. It is important to be in balance here, as the heart does need the mind as a partner to navigate and experience our physical world.

The mind is a beautiful thing for the heart to dance with in unison. When the beliefs and expectations of the conditioned mind become the master over the heart, that is when dreams dissolve, hearts break, and the incoherent patterns of your current reality are what is left. No one can truly break your heart but you. I am not discounting what it may feel like due to outside circumstances, but the actual breaking of your heart is not allowing yourself to blossom into the life you dream about and the magnificence of becoming your fullest, happiest, and healthiest potential.

> *What is your Truth?*
>
> *It is the very seat of your Soul.*
>
> *It is the Answer that lies within.*
>
> *It is the Light that shines the way to the joyous wonders of Creation.*
>
> *When darkness overshadows the purity of your Truth, you stumble onto the path that leads you away from your desired destiny.*
>
> *The world becomes a reflection of your inner disorder.*
>
> *You will know this by how you feel inside, and what you project to your world.*
>
> *As you breathe the Light and feel every cell in your*

body bathed in Love, you are once again able to access your Answers and reclaim your Truth.

As humans, you stumble.

As Universal Beings of Light and Love, you remember that you are Divinity.

Take your own hand, listen to your Soul, and gently light the way to the Truth of who you are.

— *DIVINITY SPEAKS*

Exercise 5
REFLECTION AND PATTERN RECOGNITION

It's time to start a new habit of self-observation and introspection. Reflect on your thoughts, feelings, and emotions several times a day. How often do you feel angry, unhappy, judgmental, or regretful? How often do you criticize yourself or others around you? How much do you focus on what is going wrong or what you don't have? Take notice of fear-based and negative-based thoughts, feelings, and emotions. Also take notice of love-based and positive-based thoughts, feelings, and emotions. How often throughout your day do you feel gratitude, joy, and hope? How often do you think about your blessings in life and what is going right? How often do you genuinely acknowledge your heart-led efforts, your loving nature, and your selfless service?

A good time to reflect is upon rising, around meal or break times, and before bed. This exercise takes self-reflection and complete honesty. Don't just reflect on the negative. Remember and reflect on all the positive and happy thoughts, feelings, and emotions you have. They are the emotions that really make you feel good inside. If you don't have any or just don't feel optimistic about anything right now, begin with what you are grateful for. It's okay to start with something small. There is *always* something you can find to be grateful for.

As a Transformational Life Coach and Vibrational Energy Healer, I tell my clients I understand it's not easy to immediately jump from feeling sad, angry, or hopeless to feeling happy, hopeful, or peaceful. Especially when conditions and events in our lives, or the world, feel and appear desperate, draining, or defeating. However, there is always something available in each moment to help bridge the gap.

When we begin to look at life through the eyes of gratitude and start focusing on what we have, instead of what we don't have, our perspective begins to change. I know someone who was feeling so down that he didn't know how to start feeling grateful. His mind just wasn't wired for that vibration. When it was suggested that he start with something small, he searched his mind and decided to start this exercise by being grateful for his socks. You may think this sounds silly, or why didn't he begin with something more meaningful. The point is, the simple act of declaring gratitude for something seemingly small in his life was the catalyst his mind needed in order for his heart to open to what gratitude had to offer. After several practice exercises, he had more and more things to put on his gratitude list. The more grateful he became, the more he could travel to his joy and see all the blessings in his life. It didn't happen all at once, but it did happen. The point is that once you begin this exercise, it will expand and evolve over time, and you will have more and more to put on your list. Just remember, this exercise is for you only. When we invite others to give feedback, it only gives them the opportunity to jump in and give feedback from their ego, their perspective, or their need to feel right or validated. This exercise is about reflecting on **your** thoughts and recognizing **your** patterns for **your** personal self-development. This does not mean that you shouldn't talk to anyone about your feelings. For this exercise, be mindful of what your thoughts are. Be honest with yourself. Especially if you discover that some of your thoughts or beliefs are conditioned or disempowering. Again, I encourage keeping a personal and private journal of some sort, so you can honestly write and then reflect.

You can *super-jolt* yourself into pattern recognition by using another section of the same notebook that you used for Key 1 or create a section under notes in your smartphone. Smartphones are great for quick notes or voice memos. You may not notice your patterns right away, but my suggestion is to do this daily for at least twenty-one days. The goal is to have your pattern recognition become automatic. Write down the times you catch yourself feeling, saying, or thinking something based on fear energy (anger, judgment, regret, guilt, hopelessness, envy, shame, and so on). You will also do the same when you catch yourself thinking, feeling, or saying something based on love energy (compassion, empathy, hope, support, joy, gratitude and so on).

This is a great exercise to do even when you are at work, so you can see if your patterns change between work and home. It may sound unrealistic, or sound like it may take too much time to stop and write your observations, but I guarantee this will help jumpstart you into identifying limiting emotional and thought based patterns that don't support mastering manifestation in your life.

Don't forget to read or listen to what you wrote or recorded, and then reflect on your predominant patterns. A fundamental component for change is to first become present with what you need to change. After completing this exercise you will have a greater ongoing awareness of your patterns, and how they influence your life and happiness.

You will be using this exercise, as well as the other Keys, to help transform old and self-limiting habits, into a new paradigm of attraction energy and mastering manifestation. This new paradigm is one of merging within the consciousness of infinite possibility and potential. The reality of this consciousness is already within you. It's just waiting to be recognized.

Recognizing your patterns will help set the stage for actualizing the dreams you hold most dear. This is not a twenty-one-day program to change your habits. This is a program for your entire life in which recognizing your patterns is a vital first step. It is a lifelong commitment to honoring the truth within as your guiding light to your joy, highest purpose, potential, and fulfillment.

8

KEY 4

BE READY AND COMMITTED

> *As you commit to your practice, you will begin to hear your destiny call to you within every cell of your body. You will begin to recognize the voice of Divinity within you, as it guides you to your inner peace, purpose, joy, and highest potentials.*
>
> — *DIVINITY SPEAKS*

I believe in divine timing. As with anything new, whether it is starting an exercise program, eating healthy, transforming a habit, or learning a new skill, a person must be committed and ready to change before his or her desired outcome appears. *No one can tell you that you are ready but you.* Remember, this also applies to others. You can't tell other people when they are ready either.

The way to access your highest truth and power within is through your devotion. Devotion takes dedication and discipline. If you are ready, the commitment will follow, but only if you are ready and devoted to the commitment. I know this may sound like a merry-go-round, but as with starting anything new, it is easy to fall back into old patterns of thinking and doing. Once you recognize your patterns, this will give you the information you need to consciously make changes regarding how you think and feel and what you do. As you know, your predominant energy is a vital force within the energy of conscious creation.

This is where some sort of a daily spiritual practice fits in. A daily spiritual practice helps unite you with your inner peace and neutral mind as you are guided by the light of divine inspiration. The illumination of inspiration is your catalyst for positive change. When you reach the neutral mind, through a devoted spiritual practice, destiny flows as you begin to embrace a new way of interacting and engaging with the energies of love and the harmonizing frequencies of your highest potentials.

If you are truly ready and committed, nothing will stand in your way, except for your own limiting beliefs and disempowering patterns. It is the discipline of your commitment and your devotion to recognizing and maintaining the energy of love. That is the heart and soul of your evolving consciousness. The winning formula of true and lasting happiness, success, fulfillment, and even greater health, is through your devotion and commitment to your daily spiritual practice.

You may ask: What is a daily spiritual practice? What does it look like? How do I make it happen? My answer is simply what does a daily spiritual practice mean to you? A spiritual practice has thousands of different appearances, as well as explanations. It has an infinite number of wonderful and unique ways to open and unfold within us. The commonality it shares is to break through the barriers of separation, fear, and illusion, and to unite us with the peaceful and loving presence of the Divine One within. This, in turn, helps us remember the beauty and truth of who we are as spiritual beings with infinite potentials and possibilities within our human experience. It acts as a silent reminder that we are all connected within the One Heart of the Divine Universe. A very dear teacher of mine often says, "What you focus on will grow." This is a helpful reminder to keep our focus turned inward to where we can clearly see and feel the truth behind illusions and limitations in our lives.

Wherever you are on the path of your daily spiritual practice, just know, it is not about *doing;* it is about *being*. When you unite with your being (your inner stillness that always is), you transcend the worries, limitations, fears, and frustrations of the physical world. You have open access to your inner peace and higher wisdom. There are many vehicles to help you get there. You just need to find what works best for you. Whether your vehicle is meditation, mantra, prayer, yoga, music, painting, dancing, rock climbing, jogging, skiing, horseback riding, writing, singing, or a combination of things, just remember that it *is your devotion and discipline that will carry you* to the priceless treasures that you will discover once you unite with the Divine within.

Exercise 6
YOUR DAILY SPIRITUAL PRACTICE

This exercise is simply about discovering what makes *you* light up. What gives you the most joy, peace, clarity, and purpose? Is there something you enjoy doing so much that your mind simply gives way, and you lose all track of time when you are doing it? If you don't currently have a daily spiritual practice, this is the time to identify something that calls to you from the silence of your heart, from the voice of your soul. Maybe you don't even know what that is. Maybe you do. The point is to *sit* with yourself and find out.

Personally, my daily spiritual practice includes a combination of things. The six things that are consistent are yoga, meditation, mantra, walks and bike rides with my dog, and gratitude (more on that later). These are all great *vehicles* that help me become present with my higher knowing and inner peace. The important thing is to do something *every day* that brings you to a place of blissful inner awareness which may feel outside of time.

I do some form of meditation every day, but I don't always do it sitting still. I really look at my life as a form of meditation that contributes to my spiritual practice as a whole. Becoming truly present for even a few moments is a powerful meditation in itself. If I have a day that I don't feel my practice was as committed as it could have been, I don't beat myself up about it. Most of us are not monks. We don't live a lifestyle that takes us away from the pressures of daily life. My life is a giant roller-coaster ride of ups and downs, just like yours. Circumstances change, people change, and life-altering events happen. What keeps me steady and prevents me from mentally and emotionally crashing, during changing or uncertain times, is my devotion to my daily spiritual practice. And when I do sink into a fear or negativity-based expression, within the tides of my own emotions, my spiritual practice is what I have to grasp onto. It helps me rise to a higher, more hopeful, and optimistic state of being. My spiritual practice is my lifeboat that keeps me floating, no matter what storms are going on around me. I honestly don't know how I would have continued to hold to so much positivity and hope in my heart during the COVID-19 pandemic without my spiritual practice.

A big part of my daily spiritual practice is remembering to consciously create ways to connect deeper with my heart, and connect with others as I go about my day. Besides my staples listed previously, my daily spiritual practice consists of living my life with joy, purpose, creativity, caring, and compassion. I focus on being kind, accepting, and loving. My daily spiritual practice encompasses *all* that I do. This includes activities such as yoga and meditation, but there is no limit or restriction when it comes to uniting with your own unique space or place of timelessness, connection, and inner peace. Other things that bring me to that place are helping others develop their own daily spiritual practice, writing, walking in nature, playing with my grandchildren, dancing, riding horses and motorcycles, snuggling with my husband, listening to spiritually uplifting music, or reaching out to a friend or loved one to authentically connect (not complain about what is going wrong). These are all things that connect me to the peaceful presence within the eternal moment of *now*.

What brings you there? Write it all down, and then begin devoting time to your daily spiritual practice. If you don't know what that is yet, start trying different things that have been calling to you and that you may have put on a shelf for later. The emotional roller coaster of life stays calm and steady the more you stay devoted to your daily practice. When you recognize the importance of your spiritual practice, your commitment and devotion will awaken the power and ability to unite with your happiest and most fulfilled life. Limiting or disempowering habits, behaviors, and beliefs transform as you begin to see obstacles disappear and opportunities once hidden from your former state of awareness spring forth. Your dreams are calling through the waves of timeless eternity. It may be time to start listening.

You have heard it said that practice makes perfect. That is undoubtably part of the equation. The other part is consciously attracting the *right energy* to provide the best opportunity to create your desired results. You get to choose what you want to practice in your life. You can practice a life based on love, hope, positivity, and empowerment or a life based on fear, hopelessness, negativity, and disempowerment. The glory of your radiance is the treasure within you just waiting to shine. This treasure is discovered when you powerfully proclaim your *I-am*.

9

KEY 5

PROCLAIM YOUR I AM

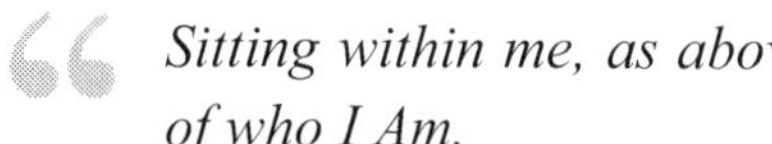

> *Sitting within me, as above, is the beauty and truth of who I Am.*
>
> — *DIVINITY SPEAKS*

I would like to ask you a personal question. What are the messages you give to the Universe every day regarding who you are? You may not think you talk to the Universe or ask any questions at all, so please allow me to offer another perspective. The Universe does not listen with ears, but it does hear the energetic communication within your thoughts, feelings, words, and emotions. It knows every aspect of who you say, think, or believe you are, and it is very generous in delivering what you ask for.

You may be thinking you did not *ask* for unsavory things or conditions to appear in your life. People don't go around asking to be fired or laid off from their job, their bank account to be overdrawn, their car to break down, or their ankle to be sprained. This is where I agree. No one would "*ask*" for such things.

As you flow within your physical experience of life, it is important to remember who *you* are, independent from the circumstances of your life, and how they show up for you. Behind your mind, your thoughts, and your beliefs, there is a presence. This is the presence you may feel when you close your eyes to the outside world and feel the connection to the energy and oneness of life. This life-force energy is an aliveness within you. Where the mind, body, and circumstances are temporary, the aliveness within you is permanent and unchanging. It is a consciousness that was there before you joined your physical body and will still be there after you depart from your physical body. When you remember the truth of your true nature, it helps amplify your predominant energy that attracts your highest purpose and greatest potentials in your physical life. The more love and positivity you radiate, the more it radiates back to you.

This doesn't mean that things you perceive as bad will never happen. We all know that bad things can happen to good people. What it does mean is that when those unexpected or unfavorable things do happen, you have a defining, strengthening force within you. You have an inner resolve that gives you support and something to hold on to so you can rise above. It gives you a strong foundation to help you from sinking lower and lower into the quicksand of hopelessness, anger, frustration, or despair. This keeps your predominant energy elevated and more positive, which gives you the advantage of maintaining the frequencies of love energy within your life.

Most of us don't place too much awareness on this presence. This is because we are so preoccupied with all the things that our minds are attached to in our physical reality, including our sense of identity. Within this identity is who we believe we are, in a world of distraction from our true inner reality.

There are infinite options on the playing field of life to feel peaceful and purposeful, or defeated and drained. The point is that you *get* to choose. You do this by the predominant energy you emit to the Universe. This is what the Universe is listening to. Your words are your wand.

WHEN YOU BEGIN TO REALIZE THAT THE MAGIC OF YOUR LIFE IS CONTAINED WITHIN THE POWER OF YOUR THOUGHTS, WORDS, AND FEELINGS YOU BEGIN TO USE YOUR WAND WISELY.

YOUR I-AM MISSION STATEMENT

When your energetic identity aligns with your dreams and desires, starting your mission statement with *I-am* is the most powerful message and one of the most valuable gifts you can give yourself. It has the ability to shape and transform your life in whichever way you decide to state it. It is important to know that the power of proclaiming your I- am will shape the outcome of your entire experience of life, whether you want it to or not.

Choose your I-am wisely, for it is the single most powerful choice of words that emanate from the energy of your thoughts. In doing so, remember that it is okay to want or desire things or circumstances, but just the desire alone will not attract those things into your life. To effectively declare your I-am, work backward from the end result of the desire. Powerfully proclaim to yourself and the Universe that you are already that of which you desire. Feel this to be true in the knowingness of your highest self within the infinite possibilities of creation.

Your inspired imagination in Key 1, along with your I-am statements sit together in partnership at the throne of your creative being. The creative being that often sits in the darkness of limitation and conditioned beliefs until illuminated with the light of your empowered inspiration. Old belief systems of lack, limitation, self-judgment, hopelessness, unworthiness, and those "I-can't" attitudes are rewritten into your new belief system of infinite possibility, abundance, fulfillment, and joy. Dormant forces within you come alive as you heartfully and imaginatively proclaim your I-am.

YOU BECOME THE MASTER OF YOUR OWN CREATIONS AS THE HIGHEST AND BEST POSSIBILITIES AND POTENTIALS OF YOUR RESONATING VIBRATIONS ARE ATTRACTED INTO YOUR REALITY.

Does this mean that you will become an NBA basketball player if you just imagine and say it is so? My answer is that it depends on where you currently are on the playing field of life. Is this a dream or goal that fits into your current possible trajectory, given your current level of desire, belief, and physical/mental abilities? I suggest to be successful in attracting your dreams, you start your I-am statements with something your conditioned mind can grasp on to. You are not trying to trick your mind, you are just reprogramming it from limited to limitless. Once you get the hang of it and your mind begins to work in partnership with your heart, you can work up to bigger things. As an example, it would be unreasonable to choose an I-am statement that you are an NBA basketball player if you have never really had the interest in basketball, or if you are five foot tall. Don't just make I-am statements unless they feel right and are guided by your heart.

Go back to review what you wrote in the "Identify Your Dreams" exercise in Key 1. We still must work within the current program of our collective agreement regarding our physical reality. In this reality, a dog is a dog, and a cat is a cat. They are what they are. They do not grow wings and fly or grow gills so they may breathe underwater. Yes, you do have superpowers of unknown and unrealized potential. Those superpowers are your own beautiful imagination that can help transport you to your most inspired, fulfilled, healthy, happy, peaceful, and purposeful life. Proclaiming your I-am is the bridge to those amazing and wonderful potentials that are already within you.

Exercise 7
YOUR I-AM MISSION STATEMENT

Write your own mission statements regarding who you are, what you do, and how you feel. Always start your mission statement with the words I-am. This is your own personal declaration to the Universe that you are already living a happy, healthy, fulfilled, and inspired life, even if it does not yet appear in your current physical or emotional perception of reality.

Use your own words for your personal mission statement. It can look something like the ones I provided below, but remember, these are only examples. You will need to create statements that will best fit *your* personal needs and desires. It can be as simple or as complex as you want it to be. Don't forget that you are always the *I- am* of whatever you think, feel, say, or write it to be.

Within your I-am statement, it is important to recognize that you understand the process of improving your thoughts *and* feelings in order to realize your dreams (even if you are not yet seeing the physical outcomes in your life yet). This is not only possible, but it is highly probable when your mind lives in partnership with your heart and you release expectation of outcome. In addition, know that the Universe always conspires *for* you with the predominant energy you radiate. Do not judge yourself if you come upon perceived obstacles that you used to call failures. These obstacles only temporarily inhibit your commitment or success. They also help lead you to alternative answers or new lessons to learn on your journey towards fulfillment.

You will always have new opportunities to practice the secret of attraction energy and consciously become the master of your manifestations. If a perceived obstacle is in the way of your dreams, try self-compassion over self-judgment. Don't forget to include your inspired imagination with your I-am statements. The dynamic energy of the 12 Keys is all interrelated. They are designed to play together as an orchestra, not a single instrument. One instrument alone may sound lovely, but it does not complete the depth, beauty, and unified harmony of the entire ensemble.

EXAMPLES OF I-AM STATEMENTS:

- I am healthy. My body feels energized, vital, and strong.
- I am peaceful. I am at peace with my past, and I am at peace with myself.
- I am abundant and prosperous in all areas of my life. I know that prosperity is a form of energy that I easily attract.
- I am grateful for my relationships, which are supportive, loving, and caring.
- I am happy. My life gives me joy and purpose.
- I am compassionate. I give myself love and encouragement as I learn a new way of relating to myself, others, and my beliefs.

- I am creative. My creativity flows from my inspiration, joy, and passion.

- I am living the life I dream of. The magic within my life grows stronger the more I follow my heart and listen within.

Just in case you are wondering, I-am statements can work any way you choose. They are not limited to attracting your highest and best potentials. Your word can be your wand for your highest aspirations and dreams, as well as your fears, judgments, and negative programming. This also includes your I-can't or I-don't statements. I have included a few I-am statements that are embedded within the vibrations of fear (negativity, doubt, and limitation). Statements and beliefs such as the ones below keep you imprisoned within your conditioned mind. It is almost impossible to break free and attract a happier, healthier, more optimistic, illuminated life when we live in the darkness of our disempowering I-am statements.

- I am not very smart or funny. People just don't seem to like me.

- I am not able to get in shape. I don't have time to exercise.

- I am always living paycheck to paycheck. I can't catch a break or find a job that I love.

- I am not lucky. Good things just don't happen to me.

- I am not attractive. No one will ever love me or want me for a life partner.

- I am not worthy of a great relationship. I am better off alone.

- I am unhealthy. I always seem to get whatever illness is going around.

- I am too old to find a life partner, go back to school, or learn a new trade. That time has passed.

THE ALL INCLUSIVE I-AM

> *I Am the One Consciousness of All That Is. I Am the One Chord, the One Song, the One Harmony, the One Universal Symphony of Resonate Vibration within you.*
>
> — *DIVINITY SPEAKS*

Proclaiming your "I-am" in life goes beyond the physical or limited universe of time, space, place, and perception. The I-am of your true inner-self never wants anything that you perceive or believe to be outside of yourself. It is only the mind or ego that clings to the belief of separation and limitation within the illusion of a fear-based reality.

We each have the opportunity to experience all of the joys, as well as the sorrows that physical life brings. We experience our realities and then hopefully learn and grow from each chapter of life. Sometimes we repeat chapters of less-than-optimal experiences until the light of our inner wisdom switches on and guides us to change our patterns. Keep this in mind as you proclaim your I-am. Not to confuse you but to help you remember the following.

YOUR I- AM IS ALL-INCLUSIVE OF EVERYTHING YOU HOLD INSIDE, AS WELL AS EVERYTHING YOU SEE OUTSIDE OF YOURSELF.

Your I-am contains the truth of the Divine Universe and the eternal, ever-present, all-knowing Infinite Intelligence within *all* things. Within this Great Remembrance, Divinity illuminates your mind with the higher vibrations of absolute love, unity, joy, and peace. It is here where true and lasting happiness resides, not anything or anyone perceived to be outside of you. I will elaborate more on this later, but for now, just realize that relationships, jobs, people, things, and circumstances cannot bring you true and lasting happiness. If that is what you are searching for to be whole and happy, you will always be searching. Yes, these things can and do contribute to a happy, joyful state of being as you experience your life. But these things all eventually pass. Only your divine inner-joy survives throughout the test of time and the truth of reality as you ascend to the Great Liberation from fear and move into the light and love of Divinity.

THE GREAT REMEMBRANCE

Fear cannot rule the minds of humankind when hearts become awakened to the Great Remembrance of love, peace, unity, and most important, truth. Keep love, faith, compassion, and grace within every thought, word, and action. The Great Liberation from fear consciousness will bring complete healing and transformation to those who see, speak, and radiate the universal language of Divine Love and Light.

— *DIVINITY SPEAKS*

10

KEY 6

DO THE WORK

Follow your heart to the highest and best feelings of desired outcomes. Your divine purpose is calling you. Remember to listen. Stay in your knowing that the energy of love will lead the way to inspired actions. Pay attention to your body, for it is the barometer for knowing what state of feeling you are in.

— DIVINITY SPEAKS

Doing the *work* may not be what you think it is. This is about working on yourself to change disempowering, limiting patterns in your life. The patterns that you may not have been aware of before reading this book and recognizing the predominant energy you hold.

It is imperative when you recognize any self-defeating, fear-based patterns that you do the work to *change* the patterns. For instance, it is not easy to replace a fear-based anger or judgment emotion with a love-based caring or gratitude emotion, because our patterns have been programmed within us for as long as we can remember. However, the more you practice this, the easier and more natural it will become.

This Key is not about working hard to achieve your goals. Doing the work means being honest and staying on top of yourself as you go throughout your day. Frequently check in to evaluate whether you are in the vibration of love or fear. Are you in judgment of someone because of how the person acts or looks or even what he or she says or believes? That is a fear-based, disempowering energy. This doesn't imply that the simple act of noticing someone who looks or acts different is disempowering or even judgmental. Life is meant to bring different flavors to the palate of our experiences. Part of the joy is noticing the various flavors of our observations. It is only when you put an association of how you think and feel about it that makes it fear-based or loved-based. There are also various times when your observations, thoughts, and feelings are neutral, somewhere in-between the domain of love and fear-based energy and emotion. The more you do the work to recognize your patterns, the more opportunities you will have to develop more evolved, self-empowering patterns that help you radiate and attract the energy of conscious creation.

Are you truly happy for someone's success in his or her promotion, even though the promotion could have gone to you? That is a love energy or an empowering energy. Even though it doesn't mean you wouldn't have loved to be promoted yourself, you are genuinely happy for your coworker, as you recognize his or her hard work and achievement.

Instead of thinking something judgmental about the scowling parent who is insensitively grumbling at their toddler who is having a temper tantrum in the grocery store, try shifting your thoughts towards compassion. I know it's now always easy when our emotions and judgments get the best of us. Just the act of feeling compassion alone can palpably change the energy field around you and radiate an invisible field of harmonious vibrations that others can pick up on. Consider for a moment that maybe the parent has not had a good night's sleep for days, or even weeks due to the many demands of a young child. Perhaps he or she doesn't have a support system at home to help cope with the trials of daily life, or parent the child more positively. Maybe he or she struggles with health, finances, or a relationship and is doing everything possible just to be at the grocery store.

In reality, whatever I think about that person doesn't really matter, for that is the story that I create. The truth of the story will most likely never be revealed to me. What matters is that I adjust my own personal judgments and feelings about the other person, while I consciously send him or her a heartfelt loving thought of peace, assurance, and hope. I can actually feel my heart reaching out to theirs while I imagine his or her heart accepting my gift through an energetic nonverbal exchange of love. You will be amazed by how love can change your initial judgmental emotion to one of a higher state. Additionally, there may be times when you feel the other person's energy elevate as well. The point is not to expect a change in them, but to notice the change in you!

THE MORE LOVE AND COMPASSION YOU FEEL, THE MORE YOUR HEART OPENS, THE MORE PEACEFUL YOU FEEL, AND THE MORE YOUR WORLD TRANSFORMS AND HEALS.

I include this practice every day as a part of my own personal living prayer. Whenever I walk by or drive by someone who catches my attention for whatever reason, I send that person a loving thought as I hold him or her in my heart. I bypass my judgments and stories as I feel my love reaching out. This only takes a moment. The more I practice this with heartfelt intention, the more I feel Divinity working through me, and I know it makes a difference. If more people would include this one thing as a daily spiritual practice, I truly believe our world would transform from the conditioned, limiting energy of fear, to the harmonious and healing energy of love. Please do not overlook the importance of remaining neutral with your judgments, feeling compassion, and sending love. It is truly the salvation our world desperately needs.

Exercise 8
STEPPING INTO YOUR COMPASSIONATE HEART

For this exercise, I would like to ask you to become consciously aware of how often you think, talk, write, post, judge, or respond about other people in negative, shameful, or disempowering ways. When you see someone begging for money at the off-ramp, what immediately comes to mind? When you see your neighbor driving by without waving or saying hello, what do you think? When someone cuts you off in traffic, how do you respond? When a person jumps in front of you at the check-out stand in the grocery store, what do you believe? When you walk by someone on the street who looks dirty or unkempt, how do you judge? When you talk to a friend about another person, how do you sound? When you post something on social media, does it inspire and uplift, or does it blame and shame? These are all basic examples to stimulate your mind to really take note of how you think, feel, speak, respond, and even write or post about others. Are your thoughts and words based on the energy of love, tolerance, and compassion, or are they based on negativity, gossip, and judgment? No one really knows the pain, suffering, or life circumstances of someone else. For some reason, people will post things about other people on social media that they would never say to that person's face. As you become more observant, you will begin to notice how you think, feel, react, and respond in all avenues of your life. You begin to recognize your personal patterns and predominant energy.

CATCHING YOURSELF IN ACTION

When you catch yourself feeling, thinking, speaking, responding, or writing something negative, disempowering, or judgmental about another person, use this opportunity to expand your energetic heart to theirs. Drop what your conditioned mind thinks it knows, and feel the love and compassion within you reaching out to his or her heart and soul. If you practice this consistently, your life truly becomes a living prayer. You will begin to automatically and energetically reach out to the highest good in the other person as you interact, pass by, talk about him or her, or post your opinions of what you think you know. You do not need to ignore what you see or pretend it is not evident, just take note and then energetically send love and compassion to that person. Your loving thoughts, intentions, and prayers will expand within you and radiate to him or her. Even though you may never know, your energetic blessing just may have made that person's day a little better! When enough of us do this consistently, this leads to a shift in our overall consciousness as we ascend to collective awakening.

This exercise is something that has the potential to be a game changer for life. When your heart opens to compassion instead of stories, the transformation that occurs within you is more powerful than I could ever describe in words. It is a primary Key to unlock your own healing, as you begin to realize that everyone suffers. No one knows the depth of another person's pain, or the complexity of how that person appears to be in the moment of your observation. You do not know the truth; you only think you do through the stories you create around your observations or the gossip or misinformation of others. When you judge others, you only dishonor and disempower yourself. When you lift others up through your love, compassion, empathy, and service, you bring the light of love to the heart of the energetic exchange. You are blessed beyond measure through the grace of the Divine.

DOING THE WORK AROUND YOURSELF

Just as you catch yourself thinking, feeling, or speaking in disempowering or negative ways about others, it is equally important to pay attention to how you think, feel, and speak about yourself. You must put yourself in the equation of feeling nonjudgmental, compassionate, and loving to truly honor yourself as an individual, who is also the expression of the Divine. When you dishonor yourself, when you undervalue yourself, when you do not like, appreciate or celebrate yourself, you are sending those same energetic signals to your Creator. You are sending signals that you are not enough, you are not important, and your life doesn't matter.

We all have years of conditioning, some more than others due to upbringing and culture, that add to our own undervaluing of self. Many times, we would not say to our worst enemy what we think about ourselves in the privacy of our own minds. Things like, I'm fat, I'm ugly, I'm stupid, I'm not capable, I'm not worthy, and I'm not good enough prevail through the conditioned and enslaved minds of humankind. Please trust me when I say that you are so much more than you believe you are. You are the glory, the radiance, the infinite potential, and the loving presence of all that is good and all that is true. You are the grace of God. You are the Universe in divine expression.

The problem is that you either don't know it, you don't believe it, or you don't know how to live it. It took years to become you. It does not have to take years to become a new, improved, happy, healthy, powerful you. When you apply the 12 Keys of Conscious Creation to your life, you are already moving the energetic mountains in your life. When you begin to live, breathe, and relate to the following exercise, those mountains may still be there, but you are the one who ascends them with the power, will, and conviction of your highest knowing. You are the one who changes the game of the conditioned mind to the truth of Divinity within you. This truth is your winning goal to magnetize, create, and sustain the life you have always dreamed of having, and be the person you have always dreamed of becoming. It's all right here, right now. It's time to step into your power and be the *you* of your destiny.

Exercise 9
THE POWER OF BELIEF

> *When your beliefs align with the knowing of The Universe, your destiny is born into reality. Choose your beliefs wisely and guide them only with a loving heart.*
>
> — DIVINITY SPEAKS

It should be no surprise that this exercise is about how you think, feel, and speak about yourself. All beliefs act as powerful magnets. The energy of your beliefs attracts resonating energy that is magnetized and then crystalized into your awareness. The crystallization process is what we see as physical reality. Stepping into the power of your belief is recognizing the fact that the energy you embody (how you think, feel, speak, and ultimately radiate) works indiscriminately toward your dreams or your fears. In reality, it doesn't care. It is your servant to help you attract and create in whatever direction your beliefs and predominant energy are pointed. When you awaken from the dream of forgetfulness, into the dream of remembrance, you begin to know (not just believe) that you have the power to be the master of how you choose to think, feel, and speak. You begin to know that mastering manifestation in the way your heart most desires through the process of conscious creation relies on your beliefs and predominant energy. The work or actions you take toward manifesting your dreams arise from this process. Things begin to make sense as you understand attraction energy in a more profound and insightful way. As you step into your power, you believe in your glory. You believe in your magnificence, your unique nature, your beauty, your strength, your will, and your gifts. We all have unique gifts that we bring to this world that are meant to be shared, appreciated, and respected. I am not talking about how others look at you, I am talking about how *you* look at you. How do you honor, respect, and appreciate yourself as an expression of the Divine?

This exercise is not something to be taken lightly or overlooked. It is vital to feel as though *you* matter. You make a difference. You light up the world. We all think of work as doing something to take action, and I'm not discounting the importance of inspired action. But, in order for inspired action to occur, you must first do the work within yourself.

To start this exercise, you will be stepping into the limitations and beliefs we all hold in the conditioned, fearful mind.

- In your notebook or on a piece of paper, write all the things you don't like about yourself. Yes, all of those things—big things, small things, ugly things, fat things, skinny things, dumb things, weak things, hateful things, hurtful things, sad things, angry things, regretful things, scary things, the list goes on. Just write without thinking and write them all down. This is for your eyes only. It is not meant to be shared. Please take your time, and do not rush through this.

- When you are done with your list, take a long look at everything you wrote.

- Next, close your eyes. Take a few slow, deep breaths, and become present within yourself. Ask within your heart this: Do these things I wrote bring me closer to truth (love and positivity) or illusion (fear and negativity)? Do they make me feel powerful or powerless? Write your answers on your paper.

- Take a few moments to reflect on your answers through the lens of your heart, without self-judgment.

- I am confident that your answers were illusions, and they made you feel powerless or less than. Correct? If you did not have this as your answer, I invite you to reread the section on love energy and fear energy.

- Please realize that illusion does not mean that the things you wrote are not seen or felt in your physical reality. They are long-held energetic patterns and beliefs that have magnetized potentials and have crystallized into your current experience of reality. Seeing them for what they are as byproducts of your belief and predominant energy give them less power to thrive in your life. As you begin to form new beliefs and elevate your predominant energy, the garden of your life begins to grow and flourish in new ways that may be beyond your current vision of understanding.

- Now close your eyes again as you take two deep cleansing breaths. Allow your heart to speak to your mind. Let your heart tell your mind that everything you wrote is not the truth. All those things are based on the energy of fear, through the belief of limitation and judgment. Therefore, they are not real, and they do not have any power over you.

- Breathe. Reflect and stay here for as long as you need to.

Allow this one simple, yet powerful statement to sink into your mind. I don't expect your mind to suddenly accept all of the disempowering things it thinks and believes about yourself to automatically shift. What I am suggesting is that you are planting a seeds for new beliefs to grow. You are telling your mind that it's belief about perceived disempowering qualities are not based on a loved-based reality, and that it is time to become open to a new belief, a fresh perspective that you are more than what you currently believe you are.

YOU ARE MORE THAN WHAT YOU SEE. YOU ARE MORE THAN WHAT YOU PERCEIVE YOURSELF TO BE. YOU ARE THE LIGHT, LOVE, AND TRUTH OF DIVINE POSSIBILITY AND POTENTIAL. YOU DESERVE TO KNOW YOUR TRUTH AND THAT YOU NO LONGER HAVE TO BE IMPRISONED IN THE ILLUSION OF FALSE BELIEFS.

This may be earth-shattering, or it may just feel like a small opening in the window of your consciousness. Whatever it feels like, anchor this moment in your heart and your mind. Recognize the ability that you have at this moment in time to revisit any belief you have about yourself. Always ask yourself is this belief based in truth (love, positivity and freedom), or in illusion (fear, negativity and limitation)?

If the belief is based on anything other than truth and love, then how can you bring yourself compassion? How can you impart non-judgment? How can you celebrate the fact that you *caught* yourself thinking in a disempowering way and then changed how you think and ultimately feel? How can you send yourself love? It is just as important (and probably even more important) to give yourself love and compassion as it is for you to send it to others. This doesn't necessarily mean that your belief or your life will change overnight, but it does open the door for transformation to be invited into the house of your subconscious mind. It is here that the belief will transform with time, patience, and self-love.

Please also do this exercise by writing down all the wonderful, positive beliefs you have, or intend to create about yourself. The I am smart, I am beautiful, I am prosperous, I am generous, I am healthy beliefs. If they come from the energy of love, they are based on truth. These beliefs are a foundation for your successful journey into the creative power of attraction energy.

If a belief is based on love, celebrate that! It is vitally important to recognize the magnificence of your true identity as you consciously attract, create, and play in this giant playground we call life. The more you acknowledge and celebrate your positive, love-based qualities and beliefs, the more high-vibrational energy is attracted to your circle of creation.

11

KEY 7

BE KIND

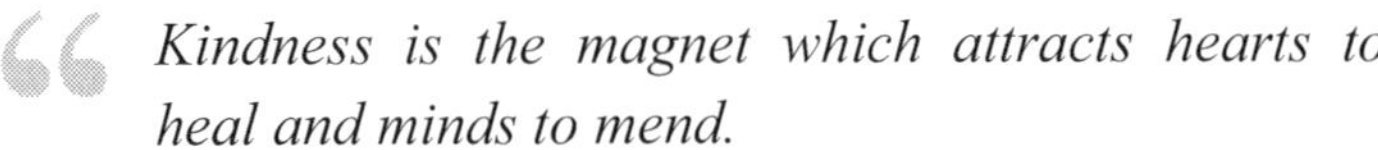

> *Kindness is the magnet which attracts hearts to heal and minds to mend.*
>
> — *DIVINITY SPEAKS*

What does kindness mean to you? I think most people would think of kindness as something they do, as in an *act of kindness*. This chapter will help you discover multiple avenues of kindness in order to help raise your energetic vibration.

Think about how you relate to kindness in your life. Not only for others, but for yourself. Do you start each day asking, "How can I be more kind, compassionate, giving, and loving?" Do you go throughout your day asking how you can be more accepting, considerate, helpful, or thoughtful and less judgmental? Most of us don't begin our days like this. We also don't generally go throughout our day in this frame of mind because we are not taught or conditioned to do so.

How about this? Do you wake up thinking about your to-do list or what you are worried, sad, angry, stressed, or depressed about? Does your day consist of believing that you know more or know better than a loved one, friend, coworker, neighbor, or stranger? Do you post judgmental or hurtful comments and opinions on social media? Do you often feel the need to be right? Do you talk about others behind their backs? Do you have disempowering, hurtful, hateful, or judgmental thoughts or words toward another person? If you answered yes to any of these, then welcome to the human condition.

With that said, all of these things have no bearing on whether you are a kind person. Kindness is an inherent quality within us. It is a virtue that most people are intimately connected to in one way or another. Just as other virtues, kindness can stealthily porpoise in and out of dormancy until nurtured and brought fully into the light of awareness. A kind person can have judgmental, hurtful, and hateful thoughts, and even actions. I personally don't know of anyone, myself included, who has not fallen into one or more of these categories at some point in life. These things or types of behaviors and beliefs do not, however, have to define us.

When we recognize a thought, belief, action, or behavior that is not congruent with our kindest and highest self, we get a chance to acknowledge it, and then change it. Your thoughts, feelings, and actions have a significant bearing on what kind of energy, people, things, and opportunities you primarily attract into your life. Holding a consistent vibration of kindness and compassion, will go a long way when it comes to your overall happiness, well-being, and connection to your inner-peace.

Now, don't confuse kindness with rolling over and allowing yourself to be someone's punching bag, literally or figuratively. Being kind to yourself can include taking a stand for your self-worth, value, well-being, and safety. It may also mean taking action to remove or distance yourself from a current situation, or using your voice to speak your truth.

Kindness is also not always being the answer to someone else's problems. As mentioned earlier in this book, it is one thing to help, and another to enable. I can't stress this enough, as I have learned this lesson the hard way a few times. You can actually do more harm than good if you continuously shelter someone from learning their own lessons in life, or if your helping is actually hurting you. You may have the best of intentions, but just realize that stealing happens in more ways than one. When you block a potential learning or growth opportunity from another person by your good intentions, you rob their lesson and possibly prolong the opportunity for that person to move to his or her next level of personal development and self-achievement. You may also be stealing your own chance to learn, grow, and be happy, as you desperately hold on to your false belief of helping. This is not being kind to yourself, or to the other person, and is actually quite the opposite.

When you question whether something you are doing is kind, ask yourself if you are helping or enabling. Ask yourself if you are contributing to, or stealing from, that person's self-growth, life lessons, or personal accomplishments. Ask yourself if you are stealing from your own happiness, health, and well-being or emotional, physical, or financial security in order to enable another.

Exercise 10

A KINDNESS LIST—INCLUDING YOU IN YOUR TO-DO

Along with doing this work in the previous Key, it is equally important to be kind and compassionate to yourself and to others. You can develop a new habit of waking up every morning in such a way that honors your need to get things done, as you include how you plan on designing your day in the kindest, most graceful, and thoughtful ways. Your to-do list should also include a *you* list.

Think about what do you need to do to honor and connect with your kindness on a more consistent basis. I suggest writing a list to help get you started. I have provided some examples to help get you started:

- How do you need to think and act to have more kindness, tolerance, acceptance, and compassion for yourself?

- What can you eat and drink that is kind to your body?

- What do you need to do to connect to your inner- peace and joy?

- How can you bring more gratitude or forgiveness to your life?

- How can you make a positive impact on others through your thoughts and actions?

- Are there any emotional, physical, or financial cords you need to cut in order to honor kindness for yourself or another person?

- Do you need professional medical, psychological, or legal services to help you gain insight, clarity, and support for a circumstance or situation?

I recommend writing your list in your journal or notebook. This is a great way to become present with what you would like to have more kindness and compassion about. Reflect on this often and change and update your list as needed.

When you inevitably catch yourself thinking or feeling something less than empowering, loving, compassionate, or joyful, be kind to yourself. Having unkind or judgmental thoughts toward yourself defeats the purpose of being a conscious creator. Remember that change is a process. If you really want to be your own masterpiece, you will need to heartfully craft your canvas of creation with the utmost truth and integrity. When you reset your thoughts and emotions to be in alignment with the peaceful presence of love, you have an opportunity to start over every moment of your day. There is always a new now, and it is never too late to begin again, regardless of your age or how many times you have tried before, or whatever your circumstances may be.

Being kind to yourself also means to treat yourself with the highest of honor, respect, and integrity. Your body really is your temple, and this temple is what allows you to love, learn, expand, experience, and serve. You are a living, breathing embodiment of Divine Intelligence (Universe, God, Source, the Unified Field, Infinite Intelligence, Great Spirit, or whatever you choose to call the Divine). Take care of yourself in all of the best ways possible. Eat healthy food, drink enough pure water, get enough rest, exercise daily, take care of yourself spiritually, spend time cultivating your creativity, speak your truth, and enjoy your passions, friends, and family. When you take care of yourself, it means that you honor your life, your purpose, and your Creator.

12

KEY 8

BE MINDFUL

> *When shades of fear are painted into the hearts of humans, their lights shine dimmer and only reflect that of which they fear.*
>
> — *DIVINITY SPEAKS*

Mindfulness is a hot topic these days. Any internet search will bring you to volumes of information regarding the importance of focusing your awareness on the present moment without attachment, judgment, or interpretation. While being present is an essential element of conscious creation, as we covered in Key 2, this is not the type of mindfulness this Key refers to.

Another component of mindfulness is to be consciously aware of where your attention goes throughout your day. This Key is threefold. Each part exists separately, yet they are united in how you decide to interact and engage with the energies of information, circumstances, and other people.

PART 1

Be Mindful of What Information You Listen to and Engage In

> *Searching for answers does not provide you with what you seek. You will become the answer when you enter into the stillness of My Presence. It is here where all things are shown to you in the awareness of your heart.*
>
> — DIVINITY SPEAKS

Think about how often you receive and relay information throughout the course of your day. This includes what you listen to, read, watch, say, and participate in. Think about your day-to-day conversations with people and your involvement with television, movies, social media, internet sites, newspapers, magazines, radio shows, and so on. Please understand that this Key doesn't mean that you shouldn't have genuine exchanges of personal or one-on-one conversations. It simply means eliminating or decreasing, as much as possible, the fear and negativity-based, disempowering *chatter* or information in your environment. You will always know what this is when you check in with your body and see how this information makes you *feel.*

In our day and age of social networking, it's disempowering to engage in low-vibrational posts or comments that promote division, anger, guilt, fear, resentment, shame, blame, judgment, or violence. If you have an opinion about something, please be kind and considerate, don't post what you wouldn't say to someone's face, or wouldn't want someone to post about you. If you really have a problem with something or someone, there are more constructive avenues to resolve your differences other than on social media. Consider the fact that you really may not know the truth about what you read, watch, or listen to, and misinformation can lead to destructive and disempowering beliefs and fear-based energy. It can also destroy reputations and lives. I'm not discouraging the exchange of information or what is important to you on social media, I am discouraging posts that promote bullying, responding in hateful, hurtful, or judgmental ways, and having the incessant need to be right in order to feel justified. This is a surefire way to defeat all the great work you have done so far. I have no problem unfriending someone on social media who feels the need to tell me how to believe or what I should be careful about believing. My truth is my truth, and my beliefs are my beliefs. If you disagree, that is fine. I will honor your opinions, but that does not mean we need to agree or engage. I encourage you to do the same on this matter.

Watching television is one of the ***most*** disempowering things you can do. The fear-based news (hint: N.E.W.S.) and pharmaceutical-driven commercials seem to dominate most mainstream media. The doom and gloom, sexually demoralizing, and overtly violent programs do nothing to raise your energetic frequency or help you stay positive. They only continue to perpetuate fear and control-based programming in the minds of society. Honestly, one of the best things you can do for yourself now is to *stop* watching *all* mainstream media, period. Replace it with other, more empowering, uplifting, and inspiring forms of entertainment or news. I have not watched the news on television for eight years (unless it's by accident as it invades my space while I am out in public), and my life has changed and improved in a myriad of positive ways that I cannot begin to describe in words.

I get information that's important to know in other ways, and then I don't dwell on something I have no direct control over.

Have you noticed the more fear broadcast on the news, social media, television programs, movies, and so on, the more hate and division is occurring between neighbors, family, friends, and society? This is not a coincidence. I'm not recommending that you live under a rock, so to say, but I suggest that you carefully and purposefully select the types of information you absorb, whether it's TV, the internet, social media, movies, magazines, newspapers, or other people. Then, be discerning about that information. Do you really *know* if it's true, or do you blindly accept information simply because it's what you've heard or read? How does that information or program make you feel? Remember that *everything* is *energy* and can empower you through love and positivity or disempower you through fear and negativity.

A HYPNOTIZED SOCIETY

As discussed in Key 2, "Be Present Now," many people in our society are glued to their personal devices. Glued is actually a nice way to say hypnotized, which, in fact, so many are. Look around when you are in a public place. How many people do you see with their heads down, seemingly mesmerized by their devices in complete disassociation from their surroundings and what is going on around them? It doesn't matter what they are looking at as they are walking, sitting, standing in line, or even driving. They are all looking at something that keeps them from being present. Their minds are occupied and distracted with the latest tragedy on their news app, the latest posts on social media, the last solicitation to buy something that came through their email, or a host of other distractions on that one little handheld computer, which we are all so very intimately tethered to. My husband, Carl, calls this the true zombie apocalypse.

Do you ever look around at all of those people with their heads down in complete unaware, mindless distraction and see just how disassociated and disconnected we really are as a society? Have you ever tried to speak to someone who is scrolling through social media and receive only short, half-present responses? Do you see entire families glued to their own devices at the dinner table, having no personal conversations? Do you ever stop to think if you are teaching your children to honor technology over conversation, or if their imaginations and initiatives have been extinguished by the immediate gratification that television, social media, or video games bring?

Have you wondered if you too are a slave to your cell phone or other technology? Don't wonder. Most of us are! This is not to pass judgment or to bring you to a state of self-doubt, regret, or hopelessness. In fact, it is quite the opposite. This is meant to help you become present and be mindful of your technology use and for you to be the example of technology use for your children.

Our devices give us an instant connection to each other, as well as immediate information on any subject one chooses to type in the search engine. The way we choose to interact and engage with our technology can lead us to liberation and union or bondage and separation. It can greatly impact the quality of our communication as well as our relationships. It's a choice not many of us really think about, but it is a choice.

I grew up in the days before cell phones. Yes, way back then. We did have answering machines from which we could get our messages at the end of the day when we came home from whatever we were doing. Aside from that, my boyfriend in college made sure I had a CB radio in my car, in case I had a breakdown on the 3-plus hour trip to visit him on the weekends. When the first cell phone was made available at a price the public could afford, I had one of those giant handheld phones that you only used in an emergency. We have come a long way since then, and as with all technology, it can be used for good or bad. It all depends on how we choose to relate to it, how we choose to use it, or how we choose to modify our use of it. It also depends on how we are teaching our children by our examples.

Exercise 11
EVALUATE YOUR TECHNOLOGY USAGE

I have a little exercise for you that will open your eyes if you choose to try it. My husband, Carl, did this first as an experiment and has since decided to adopt it into his life. He was noticing that he was spending too much wasted time on social media on his cell phone. Honestly, I was noticing it as well. As I mentioned previously, our usage of technology can have its place as something that unites and connects or distracts us from being present. Specifically, social media has an alluring draw that pulls you in and keeps you there. It actually was designed to do that. It has a way of preventing those who habitually engage on its various platforms from being positive, productive, or free-thinking.

Carl became aware of the fact that whenever he went to check his social media or to post something, whether it was business or personal, he also got sucked in (as many of us do) to scrolling through the newsfeed. He slowly began to notice that this was not only a nonproductive use of his time, but it took him away from doing and experiencing other things that are in the here and now. It took him away from being truly present.

His plan was a deliberate and decisive one. When he realized his addiction to social media, he removed all social media from his cell phone. I know this sounds drastic, but if you try it, you may see just how addicted you are. Carl did not give up on social media entirely; he just created his own terms of use. He still set time aside several times a week to sit down and check his social media or post from his laptop computer for business purposes. In a sense, he took control of mindless distractions by scheduling time throughout the week to sit down and be present with his social media. His time spent on social media is now purposeful, meaningful, thoughtful, and self-regulated. I have since tried this as well, and the renewed sense of expanded time and freedom is priceless. Not to mention that there are now more precious moments to be present with other things and people in my life.

I know not everyone has the luxury of having a computer, and some social media apps only allow you to post from your cell phone or iPad, but I still suggest trying this for a minimum of a week or more, just to determine how many times a day you reach for that social media fix. Maybe this will help you break a disempowering habit and build a new empowering one.

If you can't bear to remove the apps, I suggest becoming present with how many times a day you *pop in* on your social media and anything related to time spent on your cell phone. Keep track of it in your journal or the notes on your smartphone.

My best suggestion is to schedule times during your week (preferably routine set days and times) to be present with your social media and do what you need to do for business or otherwise. This will help prevent you from being a prisoner of your own cell phone. And remember, it's not only social media that keeps us distracted and hypnotized. Whether your distraction is the news app, games, cryptocurrency, stocks, or anything else like texting or emails, then take note accordingly of how much time you spend on your electronic devices. You then have the information to modify your relationship and the time you spend with your technology in a conscious and aware way. Is it helping you or hurting you? You can retrain your brain to self-regulate as you take your life back and have more time to be present now.

PART 2

BE MINDFUL OF WHO YOU SPEND YOUR TIME WITH

> *Do not waste your purpose on ugliness, deception, control, and division. Unite as you were meant to unite, awaken from the slumber of deception into the truth of reality, and know that every light that shines brighter contributes to the reflection of the whole.*
>
> — DIVINITY SPEAKS

Friends, family, coworkers, and acquaintances who live their lives dominated and suffocated by fear-based thoughts and emotions are toxic and they are detrimental to the success of your mission. This doesn't mean to sever relationships with those you care about and are not on the same path as you. But it does mean to be mindful of your own need to rejuvenate and recharge independently of them, whoever *they* may be. Moving forward, develop a strategy for interacting with these people if they mean that much to you. Some of them will naturally fade away as you begin to vibrate at a higher frequency. When this occurs, and it will, you will start attracting friends who vibrate more harmoniously with you. Sometimes family, friends, and coworkers will also begin to vibrate at higher levels just from being around you.

Although it is possible, don't expect grand changes in others. Not all people are ready or open for change, and they really do prefer (whether they say it or consciously know it) to remain down in the trenches. You may have the biggest heart in the world, and you may be the most compassionate of anyone you know, so I'm not saying don't lend a hand or help someone who is down. Compassion for others is a very high vibration, and in times of turmoil, it can bring peace to a troubled heart. It takes a great deal of discernment when it comes to knowing the difference between helping and enabling. There is also a phrase—and I'm sure you have heard before—which is, "everything happens in its own time." Remember that everyone is on their own journey and must walk their unique paths to learn specific life lessons. It's not up to you to force change in others or make something happen before its time. Persistent enabling may actually steal the experience of valuable life lessons. This also leads to an endless cycle of codependence, fear, and despair.

The people who are meant to stay in your life will still be there. The more you accept who they are on their own journey, the more peace you will have, whether they remain physically in your life or not. The people who are ready and open to change will find their way. Maybe that way could be just from being inspired by the beautiful changes they see in you.

Allow yourself to be free in your thoughts, open in your beliefs, and clear in your understanding of the Divine. The freedom of this understanding lies in the truth of knowing no person or situation as either good or bad; it is the perception through the lens of your reality. You are not here to be "right." You are here to participate, as your Soul is

designed to do for your own development and contribution. Take the burden of judgments and criticism and place them aside. In doing so, you are set free to discover a new reality in which the truth of who you are becomes more important than changing or judging the ways of others.

— *DIVINITY SPEAKS*

Exercise 12
BE PRESENT WITH OTHERS

This exercise is simply to become present with how you feel when you are around friends, family, coworkers, and acquaintances. How do you feel when you interact with people in person, via email, on the phone, video calls, through text, and on social media? How do you feel when you meet someone new for the very first time? Pay attention. With practice, your inner barometer will tell you the energy people in your life emit, as well as how you feel when you interact with or even think about them. If it doesn't feel good, something needs to be adjusted. The adjustment could be that you need to reevaluate how they fit in your life, or if they still fit into your life as you are opening to a new positive and powerful belief system. The adjustment could be you need to accept them just the way they are and stop trying to change them. You may consider to simply modify your responses in all forms of communication to one of a higher vibration. You may also wish to set boundaries. Other adjustments could mean that you need to stop enabling or that you simply need more space. Maybe you need to take a stand for yourself as you step into your power and honor your self-worth.

This is not about telling people what is wrong with them. This is about becoming present with what *you* need from the relationships in your life, as you are honest with your communication and speak your truth. Do the relationships serve you, or do they not serve you? Do you feel empowered, joyful, grateful, supported, and peaceful around them, or do you feel depleted, stressed, angry, unworthy, powerless, worried, or anxious? Remember, this is not about them. This is about you. You can energetically discern which relationships lift and empower you and which ones do not. The fact is that some relationships that don't appear to serve us are family, friends, or coworkers who we are committed to, or compelled, for various reasons, to stay in relationships with. Some of our most difficult relationships to navigate can be with family members or significant others. They can continue on and on for years with the same broken record or the same depleting patterns. Evaluating relationships through the lens of a new belief system can feel unsettling as you search for the answers from your highest self. Trust in your process. When you receive answers from your heart, you will know what is true for you.

There may be karmic lessons for certain people to be in your life. Don't dismiss that possibility. Altering relationships is not some thing to be taken lightly, so please think carefully about how you proceed. If you decide that a relationship in your life needs to be restructured or severed, do it with the utmost compassion. Always remember to honor yourself in the process. If you are being hurt, taken advantage of, used, neglected, or abused in any way, it is time to save yourself. It may take some professional help for you to fully see this and develop a plan of action. If you see yourself in an unsafe or dishonoring situation, I urge you to get help. Please believe me when I say that you are worth it.

PART 3

BE MINDFUL ABOUT SHARING YOUR SECRET TOO SOON

One of the easiest ways to dampen your progress towards mastering manifestation is to share your *secret* about how you are achieving your remarkable successes too soon. This is imperative, as people who are not ready to believe this actually works, will not be able to accept or understand your new strategies until they are ready. It is not for you to tell them they are ready.

I advise discernment in this area to protect your new way of thinking and being until you know your new beliefs and methods of attracting your dreams into reality are sitting on a solid foundation within you. The doubt that cynical or skeptical energy and opinions can instill is detrimental to your progress of uniting with your highest joy and most purposeful life. It can actually make you question the wonderful things that you see are happening to you as a result of applying the Keys of Conscious Creation in your life. Some may be jealous of your new outlook on life and all of its blessings. They may chastise you or react in an argumentative manner because they don't understand or believe in the Law of Attraction. Remember, it's up to each individual to recognize when they are ready and then commit to change. No one can do that for them. They must do it themselves. If you immediately start telling someone *how* you've changed or how you've become happier, healthier, less stressed, more fulfilled, more abundant, and so on, it may lead them to convince you that you're blessed because of other reasons or why you are wrong in your beliefs. You may have blessings in your life (things, people, circumstances) for other reasons, but believe me when I say that those other reasons are all interconnected within your circle of attraction energy and the new belief system you are developing. I have seen relationships strained due to the need to be right and not being open to the Keys of Conscious Creation. No one likes to have their beliefs challenged. You could certainly give them a copy of this book to spark their interest, but please do not push it on anyone. There is actually truth in the saying you can lead a horse to water, but you cannot make him drink. Believe me, I have actually tried this, and it is true.

If you feel compelled to share your *secret*, then do it in a way that honors your journey and the journey of others. For instance, if you really wish someone to become inspired by what you know to be true, then share in a way that discloses the information slowly. See and feel how the person reacts to what you are sharing. If at any time you discern the feeling of unauthentic interest or skepticism, then stop immediately and politely change the subject. Compassionate people always want their family and friends to hop on the train of happiness, higher awareness, and self-fulfillment. Just remember that everyone has their own journeys through the course of their lives. Sometimes the destination is different than yours.

RESTORING YOUR VISION

When you see the world through the eyes of the conditioned mind, all fears play into the perception of your vision. The fears of others become your own as your mind thinks it believes what it sees. We are here to remind you that you are here to look beyond what you think you see. Look beyond, into the truth of Reality, by opening your awareness to the infinite possibilities of Creation. Know that your vision is restored when your capacity to unlearn the conditioning of your senses allows you to see through the eyes of your heart and wisdom of your Soul. Looking through the eyes of Truth restores not only your vision but also the unlimited potential of your purpose here in this time and place. Question everything you believe you see from the eyes of yesterday. Your new vision will give you lessons, truth, and insights to flow within the steam of Inner Wisdom and Higher Knowing.

— *DIVINITY SPEAKS*

13

KEY 9

BE FORGIVING

> *Forgiveness holds the healing energy of the Universe within the grace of your heart.*
>
> — *DIVINITY SPEAKS*

Forgiveness is the root of all healing and the cornerstone of your magnetic qualities—forgiveness of self, forgiveness of others, and forgiveness of situations, events, and circumstances. Without forgiveness, pain and suffering run as the silent and corrosive undercurrent of an otherwise happy life. One cannot be truly happy, fulfilled, or at peace when there is something left unforgiven. When you truly forgive, you let go of the blame, anger, and judgment for whatever it is that you did or someone else did. You let go of things that have happened or may still be happening.

Forgiving does not mean that you must forget. Whatever happened is part of your personal story. One in which you now have the opportunity to learn and evolve from. It is important that you learn from the lessons as well as from the pain of your personal story. It's equally critical that you learn how to release the pain that stems from feelings of anger, sadness, guilt, blame, resentment, or hatred, so it doesn't become the repetitive highlight of your personal narrative. The highlight should be the lessons learned and the gifts ultimately received. When you hold onto the pain, anger, shame, or blame, you retain the emotional and psychological energy that prevents you from healing and moving forward. You may never fully understand why something has happened to you or someone else, but you can expand into a higher level of forgiveness, and ultimately learn from your experience. If you need to, please go back and reread "Emotions as Teaching Tools" in chapter 4 to review the importance of feeling your emotions.

When you truly forgive, you allow the energy of unconditional love to transform the pain that is associated with anger, blame, shame, hatred, resentment, or guilt. The crushing power of these thoughts and emotions holds the vibration of fear energy in your life. The lack of forgiveness may also be compromising your ability to have an honest relationship with your other virtues. Holding on to disempowering thoughts and feelings blocks your connection to the life-affirming gifts of character, such as compassion, kindness, understanding, peacefulness, and strength.

When you truly forgive, you feel lighter. You breathe easier. You feel restored, as the consuming pain within your heart is gracefully transformed into a neutral or peaceful state, through the grace of unconditional love. You feel the inspired potential of your life force energy grow stronger. You feel as if there is more space within you for other virtues, such as gratitude, joy, faith, hope, and peace to flourish and thrive within the garden of your life.

If there is one thing I could tell you about healing your heart, I would ask you to forgive. The moment you have truly forgiven, your heart is released from the bondage and burden of oppression and expands into the illumination and love of the knowing soul. It is here that true healing happens.

> *If you want healing for yourself, you must live in the peace of who you are. If you want healing for others, you must live in the surrender of who they are. It is impossible for one healing to be complete without the other.*
>
> — *DIVINITY SPEAKS*

THE ENERGY OF FORGIVENESS

The energy of forgiveness is one of the most restorative vibrations for your health, happiness, and inner peace. It is also one of the most challenging vibrations to truly become present with. When we, or someone we love has been hurt, let down, demeaned, blamed, shamed, or victimized, forgiveness is not something we immediately go to. In fact, anger, rage, or even hatred may be the first emotions we experience. We also can have many layers of emotions as we go through the healing process of forgiveness. How often have you thought that you had forgiven someone or something only to discover a few days, weeks, or even years later that you are still suffering, after you thought you had forgiven? This is not uncommon, so please don't feel that this only happens to you. I have also been through the revolving door from blame and anger, to forgiveness and compassion, only to have something trigger inside me after I thought I had healed. It takes patience, practice, and compassion for true forgiveness to be found. I'm not talking about the lip service when you *say* you have forgiven. I am referring to the genuine *feeling* of forgiveness that only comes as you unite with your grace within. Please don't judge yourself if or when you are triggered. Allow yourself to honor your feelings, and then begin the forgiveness process again. It is here where you step into your grace.

Exercise 13
FORGIVENESS

I have practiced this exercise several times. Each time has been quite profound and liberating. After completion, I feel lighter. I feel as though I have more open space within my heart. I can breathe deeper and no longer feel the oppressive weight of anger, blame, or bitterness. Whether you need to forgive someone else or yourself, this exercise can completely transform your heart from a place of suffering, to a place of neutrality, acceptance, and peace. The exercise is meant to be done after you have completed the Be Present Now Meditation and the Heartful Breathing Meditation in Key 2. When you connect to the present moment and are in a state of inner-peace, this exercise will act as a bridge to your forgiveness.

- Begin by sitting quietly in a space where you are away from other people, and you feel safe and comfortable.

- Close your eyes.

- Take a long, deep inhalation through your nose and feel the air enter your lungs and expand into your abdomen. Pause for a moment, and then exhale through your nose. Hold your exhale for another moment until you feel the natural urge to inhale again. Continue to do this for at least five breaths. Stay heart-focused, as you were in your Heartful Breathing Meditation. As you breathe deep and slow, you will begin to feel calm and centered. Please do what you are comfortable with.

- Continue breathing at your own pace and comfort. Try to keep your breathing long, slow, and even. Keep your eyes closed. Pay attention to relaxing your jaw and the space between your eyebrows. Feel your shoulders drop and relax.

- Begin to think about something or someone you have not forgiven. It may even be yourself. Stay heart-centered. Keep your jaw and shoulders relaxed, as well as the space between your eyebrows.

- As you remain heart-centered, take a few minutes to become present with the peace within. Remind yourself that you are safe and protected, and that nothing can harm you.

- In your mind's eye, see the person or situation you would like to forgive. If you need to forgive yourself, then imagine yourself in your mind's eye. For this example, we will use another person. You may wish to view the event or circumstance in your mind's eye, as if you are watching from a distance or watching a movie. If you have been the victim of a violent crime and/or if you are not comfortable facing the object of your forgiveness, please withhold this exercise until you speak to a mental health professional, or practice this exercise on something less traumatic.

- Bring the object of your forgiveness as close to you as you are comfortable with. If you are not able to see the person in your mind's eye, that is okay. Just pretend that he or she is there, and you are looking at him or her.

- As you bring the person closer in your mind's eye, pay attention to how you feel. Keep up with your slow, rhythmic, relaxed breathing. Do not rush the process. Stay here for several minutes or longer as needed.

- Now begin to imagine and feel that person's soul is standing right in front of you. Remind yourself that this is not the physical person, and there is nothing that can physically or emotionally hurt you. You are present with the divinity of his or her soul.

- Keep in your heart-space. Continue with slow, deep, and rhythmic breathing.

- This is your opportunity to look past the imperfection of the physical, and into the perfection of the soul. You look past what he or she did, or did not do. You are looking past the personality and the ego. You are looking at that other person as the grace of God. You are looking past the pain, past the anger, past the emotion. Even if the physical aspect of that person would not ask for forgiveness, know that his or her soul would.

- Keep breathing. Stay focused in your heart-space.

- Stay here for several minutes as you maintain your connection with the perfection of that person's soul from your heart-space.

- Now begin to energetically reach out to that person from the loving presence of your heart. You may even want to physically extend your arms if you are compelled to do so. Look deeply into his or her eyes, or imagine your soul sending light and love to his or her

> soul. Repeat the following out loud until you feel a shift: "I forgive you. Please forgive me. I love you. Thank you."

This will take several minutes or longer. Imagine and feel the words you are speaking being lovingly and gracefully accepted by that person's soul. Repeat the mantra even if you do not think there is anything *you* need to be forgiven for. It's okay if you do not love or even like this person. This exercise is for the benefit of *your* healing process. You are not connecting on a level of the imperfections of the mind, body, or actions of that person. You are connecting on a level of the truth, beauty, and perfection of the soul.

Once you feel the shift, you will know it. Stay present. Once you feel the shift, don't abruptly stop the exercise. By this point, you may have tears streaming down your face, or you may be sobbing with released emotions. This is okay. Healing happens in your tears, as well as the release of your emotions and the transformation of your pain, blame, resentment, or anger.

When you feel you are ready to stop, take a nice long, deep, cleansing breath. Feel the peace of forgiveness and unconditional love filling your entire body. Exhale. Exhale the pain. Exhale the suffering. Continue to inhale your peace, and with each exhalation, feel yourself getting lighter. Feel the weight lifting as you are able to breathe deeper. Feel more room in your heart for love and peace. Feel the true radiance of your grace within, as you join with your forgiveness, and feel the glory of a new beginning.

Gently stretch your arms, roll your neck, and breathe in the feeling that arises in your heart that forgiveness brings. Be present with this feeling. This is a time for self-reflection. Be reverent and in deep gratitude for this soul-to-soul interaction.

You may want to wait to discuss this with anyone until you have had time to process and feel ready.

Do not think that you have to like the person or be involved in that person's life to forgive and heal. Forgiveness does not mean you need to approve of that person's actions, behaviors, beliefs, attitudes, or lifestyle. That person may still be a horrible person who still does awful things. The forgiveness that you needed was in the spiritual realm. It was soul-to-soul perfection of infinity to perfection of infinity. The depth of your healing lies in the ability to forgive at this level. When you have shifted, you will know.

It is important to understand that true forgiveness doesn't always occur instantaneously with this exercise. You may have deep, painful and emotional scars or wounds from psychological suffering that you have physically, energetically, or psychologically held onto. You may need to repeat the forgiveness exercise after some integration and reflection, until you feel that shift. If you don't feel the shift yet, please do not judge yourself or think you have failed. Allow yourself grace and compassion. The situation may be too fresh, and you may be too emotionally wounded at this moment in time to fully forgive. We all have the opportunity to learn lessons from our pain and suffering. You may have some lessons from your pain that still need to be processed before they are let go. It could be that much time has passed, and your patterns of pain are too embedded in your consciousness. Everyone breathing experiences different levels of emotional distress over the course of a lifetime. This may mean getting professional help, which I will go into more detail later. I believe in divine timing. I invite you to do the same. When the time is right, and you have fully stepped into your forgiveness, you will become liberated from your suffering.

14

KEY 10

BE GRATEFUL

> You can always be happy if you choose to be. Love is the way when you walk in gratitude.
>
> — *DIVINITY SPEAKS*

Feeding the garden of your everyday life with gratitude is the nourishment you need to strengthen, and sustain the magnetic forces of attraction energy. It's important to think thankful thoughts, as well as feel grateful as much as possible. How do you do this? It's easier than you may think, but is so often overlooked. When you give thanks, every step of the way, for the big as well as the little things, you are planting the seeds to grow and ultimately attract more things to be grateful for. It's really so simple, but this Key is often neglected when current situations appear dismal, or you have fallen down the rabbit hole of fear-negative-based living. Just remember that one aspect or condition of your life should not discount or devalue other things that provide beauty, love, support, nourishment, shelter, and so on. You just need to remember where to focus your predominant energy, and start again if you have *fallen*. We all fall, so don't think you are alone or that you can't find anything to be grateful for. If you start small, your gratitude garden will grow with the proper care and attention.

Gratitude, along with forgiveness, is one of the highest and most empowering frequencies known. There is a common saying: "If you can't run, be grateful you can walk." This is an excellent reminder to look for the positive in any situation, and bring your gratitude with you wherever you go (walking, running, or anything in between). Being in a state of gratitude is vital for the right kind of energy to attract to you. Being in a state of gratitude also helps keep you in the flow of uniting with the highest and best outcomes in your life.

Gratitude is a vibration that has its own unique qualities of opening one to attracting positive outcomes in life. The true magnetic nature of gratitude depends on uniting the two forces of *being* grateful (mindfully), and *feeling* grateful (heartfully). Think of it this way: someone can say they are grateful, but not really *feel* the gratitude within. While this type of gratitude is a starting point, the magnetism for attraction is weak. The nature of this level of gratitude needs cultivation from the heart to fully express the beauty of its gifts. The more you *feel* the beauty of the blessings within the energy of gratitude, as they expand within you, the greater the magnetic quality of your gratitude grows in strength and power .

Gratitude can easily be overlooked when life appears to be going against us, instead of for us. Many of my clients come to me during times of great turmoil, pain, and suffering. For some, practicing gratitude is too far up the ladder for their current ability to climb. They look at gratitude as something they hope to *get to* later, after their current life challenges are overcome or resolved. Some feel that world situations or loss of health, wealth, or loved ones, prevent them from ever truly being happy, healthy, or fulfilled again. I have deep sympathy for these clients, as I realize that in most situations, the challenges they come to me with, have been going on for months, or in many cases, years. They have tried countless conventional and alternative care and treatment options, and are at a place of feeling completely and utterly helpless and defeated. The joy of life has long since been removed from their daily experience, as they battle the deep and dark forces of hopelessness and depression. During vibrational energy healing sessions, and transformational life coaching, the loving presence of gratitude is the energy I continually connect with to help my clients access their deepest peace and highest healing.

On the flip side, being grateful as a daily practice is also commonly overlooked when things are going well. If you are currently experiencing good health, do you feel thankful on a daily basis for your good health, or do you only feel grateful for your health after you recover from an illness? When you have a job that pays your bills, do you give thanks for that job (whether you like the job or not), or do you only feel grateful when you get another job after a period of unemployment? If you have a family or a partner who is loving, caring, and supportive, do you give thanks for them everyday, or do you only give thanks after something has happened and you remember how lucky you are to have meaningful relationships in your life? Do you wake up every morning thankful that you have the opportunity to experience another day, or do you immediately begin to stress and worry about what you can't do, what you don't have, or what isn't fair?

In all sincerity, I'm not discounting if you are in pain, or sick, or someone you love is hurting. But starting your day ruminating on what is going wrong, will only invite more of the same. It does nothing to lift you up. Remember earlier in the book when I said I have a friend who was feeling so defeated he couldn't find anything to be grateful for? He started with his socks, and then worked up from there. We always need a starting place, and we always have a new moment to begin the process of gratitude.

I think it is part of human nature to take our everyday lives for granted. As I write this, our entire world is experiencing the effects of COVID-19, the greatest global pandemic of known history. The things I used to take for granted, like going out to dinner or walking on the beach were not allowed until just recently. As of this writing, in many states, those things are still forbidden. Regardless of how the world around you seems to be, what we do or don't do, and can or can't do, there is always something to be grateful for. There is always that next level of appreciation to reach for, as we elevate up the ladder of genuine gratitude.

We often don't think about how fortunate we are just to be alive. I would like to ask you to just pause for a moment. Think about the fact that you are alive right now. This is something we often take for granted. We don't remember or reflect upon the fact that our lives are sacred gifts. Life as we know it can be here one moment, and be gone in the next. We never really know when our next breath will be our last. This is not to put fear into you at all, but quite the opposite. This is to help you unite with the vibration of gratitude for every precious life-giving breath you take, and then make the most of what you have right now.

Now, take a deep breath and feel the air gently and deeply filling your lungs. Feel the harmonizing energy of gratitude infuse your body with each inhalation. Imagine and feel the release of fear-based thoughts such as hopelessness, anger, or judgment, with each exhalation. This one simple practice is so powerful that it can literally change your day and even your life. It can remove obstacles from your mind as your heart is open to receive the gifts of the divine Universe.

TRUE GRATITUDE

The vibration of true gratitude transcends thought, and emotion. As you begin to unite with this level of gratitude, it takes on a life all its own. Flowing within the stream of all things, its availability depends on the awareness and receptivity of the receiver. Universal and ever-present, gratitude exudes its radiance from within.

When you touch the divine essence of true gratitude, your experience of its virtue is forever changed from unknowing to knowing. As the moments build, you will have the next opportunity to become aware and connect again and again and again.

As the muscle of your etheric memory strengthens, you begin to remember from a place of non-mind and non-thinking, that the consciousness of gratitude is your very own loving nature. It contains the seeds of your deepest peace and highest joy that opens to the love and light of your Soul.

As you learn to be grateful in every moment, you will begin to unite with your destiny. Doors will open, opportunities will arise' obstacles will transform physically, mentally, emotionally, and spiritually. Dormant forces within will guide you to the next best way of self-discovery and inspired action for growth, service, and renewal.

The energy of true gratitude continually transforms fear-based thoughts and feelings toward the supreme loving and ever-present truth of Divine

> *Consciousness. Gratitude brings you back home, to your true and loving nature.*
>
> — *DIVINITY SPEAKS*

If you have a hard time being or staying *in* gratitude, then begin slowly. Remember that Rome was not built in a day, and it may take time to reprogram your brain. Place your awareness on being grateful for the little things in your life, such as the delicious, healthy lunch you had or the perfect cup of coffee you may be enjoying right now. Maybe you are grateful because it's not raining today or you have a well-deserved day off from work. Perhaps you are grateful because you found twenty dollars in your coat pocket, or an old friend called, one you haven't spoken to in years. You can work up to bigger or more profound things, but the key is that you are, in essence, starting to retrain your brain to think and feel differently. If you catch yourself being drawn back into the seductive pull of thinking disempowering thoughts, don't beat yourself up. Give yourself a pat on the back for catching yourself in action, and then reset your thoughts. After a while, this will become easier and easier, and soon it will become automatic.

Remember to include the creative powers of your inspired imagination. Give thanks, and *feel* your desired outcome as though it has already happened. Don't allow your mind to tell you that what you are grateful for is not in your life, or not possible to achieve. The magnetic energy of the outcome is there. It just may not have materialized physically in your life yet.

Exercise 14
GRATITUDE AND YOUR INSPIRED IMAGINATION

The power of gratitude united with your inspired imagination is unparalleled when it comes to magnetizing the life of your dreams. There are a number of ways to connect with what you hold most dear—what you count as your blessings in life. A gratitude journal is a great place to start. Everyone has heard of a diary. A gratitude journal is much like a diary, only instead of writing accounts of your day, you will list all the things you are grateful for—big, small, and in-between. There is no limit and no end to all the blessings in your life.

As you meditate on your gratitude list, begin to notice how the vibration of gratitude feels in your body. Does it make you feel lighter, more expansive, peaceful, or calm? Maybe it takes your awareness to a place where you feel more hope and joy. It's OK to imagine how gratitude speaks within you while learning a new way to perceive information. Gratitude has a universal language of vibration and feeling, which the heart can hear. As you become more present with gratitude, your heart will begin to translate the unspoken messages so your mind can understand.

THE FEELING IS THE SECRET *AND* THE KEY TO ACCESSING THE MAGNETIC QUALITIES HELD WITHIN YOUR GRATITUDE AND INSPIRED IMAGINATION.

As genuine gratitude for all things, big and small, becomes a daily habit, it provides energy and fuel for your spiritual practice. It helps close the doors of lack and limitation, while opening the doors of possibilities and potentials that you may not have noticed before. You will be amazed at how perceived obstacles seem to melt away, while new opportunities arise. You will see things in a different light, or may be guided to take action in ways you have never considered. As you unite gratitude with your inspired imagination, you will have taken an enormous leap into mastering manifestation in a glorious and magnetic way.

You may want to revisit the exercise in Key 1 titled "Journey into Your Imagination, and Feel your Dream Fulfilled" to remember just how important it is to unite your imagination with gratitude.

> *Be in humble gratitude for all things. It is in this awareness that your consciousness awakens to the Truth of Divinity. It is in the knowing of this Truth in which you attract what you radiate. What you most reflect becomes the endless manifestations of your reality.*
>
> — *DIVINITY SPEAKS*

15

KEY 11

GET SUPPORT

> *Asking for help is not admitting defeat. It is making a statement to the Universe that you are ready to rise above your current situation and that you are worth it.*
>
> — *DIVINITY SPEAKS*

Don't think you have to do all of this alone. If you are one of more than three hundred million people in the world who are estimated to suffer from depression, my heart goes out to you. Like many people, I have experienced periods of depression throughout my life. I also have family members who have struggled with devastating, life-altering chronic and postpartum depression. It is incredibly heart-wrenching to witness, especially when you know there is nothing you can do to help other than to be there and love the person. A very dear person who has experienced depression once reminded me that there is nothing worse than someone trying to tell you to think positive thoughts and have positive feelings when you are depressed. They are entirely right about this, especially when the information is not invited or sought out by the receiver.

This book is not about replacing your traditional medical care or suggesting a quick fix to change your life. As a holistic healer, I know that complete and spontaneous healing can and does occur. I have witnessed healings in my practice that have mystified the medical professionals and have turned the most hard-core skeptics into believers. However, we must remember that patterns of thought, emotional triggers to stress, fear-based thinking, and imbalances in mind, and body typically take time to develop. They can become deeply ingrained habits or ways of thinking and believing that are not easy to transform after years of cementing into our belief systems. There are also genuine situations that occur spontaneously, such as the death of a loved one or experiencing a life-altering event, that can trigger depression. Healing from anything, whether physical, mental, emotional, or spiritual, requires unique tools, time, and effort from the individual. This healing often requires support from others, whether they are friends, family, coworkers, or medical professionals. There is no shame in seeking out a reputable, qualified medical or mental health professional to help you navigate what type of medical help or services will suit your individual situation the best.

The ideas in this book are supplemental to whatever medical services, tools, care, or support you currently have. There are other people out there who can relate to what you may be going through, but finding the right kind of support is paramount. Think about family or friends you feel comfortable reaching out to. Please don't be embarrassed or ashamed to open up to people who love you or you feel connected to. Part of your healing journey is removing yourself from self-isolation and having the courage to speak up. We often don't want to share our darkest times with others due to feeling self-conscious, unworthy, ashamed, or afraid. As human beings, we are meant to thrive in a community. Find your community, so you don't have to feel alone. Some ideas are to find a positive, uplifting spiritual community, community center, or group to join. More and more things like this are also opening up online. You can also find like-minded people and events in your area through various social media outlets and spiritually oriented publications. Also, don't hesitate to ask around. Sometimes old-fashioned word of mouth is the best resource out there.

A REMINDER ABOUT MINDFULNESS

One of the best things about discovering how powerful your feelings are in attracting the life you wish to create, is sharing your "ah-ha" moments and personal revelations with other like-minded people who are also on a spiritual journey. Just remember to be mindful. I don't recommend going into detail about all of your new discoveries with others, unless they ask. And even then, be mindful about how much you share until you establish a feeling of mutual trust, understanding, and respect. If you feel you need more than just social support, please do not hesitate to talk to a qualified counselor or medical professional. Sometimes talking about your feelings can provide the most profound insights and personal healing.

FROM VICTIMHOOD TO VICTORY

Keeping a journal can be your best asset during this time. A journal will help you keep a record of your *I-am* statements, your predominant energy, your dreams, your gratitude, your spiritual practice, pivotal moments, daily renderings, and ongoing revelations. It will also help you see the progress you make or don't make over time. It will show if you repeat the same patterns with different people or situations. I know this to be true on a personal level. My journals have provided the wake-up call I needed more than once to move beyond the cycle of abusive or destructive relationships. It helped me identify my own limiting beliefs and self-defeating behaviors when I allowed my power to be hijacked by the manipulation or deceit of another. My journals also helped me see when I was not honoring my path towards my purpose in life.

When I look back on my journals, I see a woman who was blinded by the light of her own misplaced compassion—a woman who believed enabling was helping, while allowing herself to be victimized and abused in some situations. I now celebrate victory over these self-defeating beliefs and behaviors. My success was accomplished as I began to truly honor my purpose and self-worth and walk in the light of my own truth, power, and love. And yes, I did get help in a few situations, which provided much needed support and guidance during times of fear, doubt, and obscurity. I am not sure if I would have seen or done what I needed to do to be triumphant without it. I changed my habits of thinking, believing, and, consequently, acting. I changed my life from victim to victorious. I am only saying this because if I can do it, so can you.

Exercise 15
TAKE CONTROL

Think about where you may need support and in which way. Write this down. Be truthful with yourself. When you are honest with yourself, you are ready to face your situation and take control of your life.

Are you in a situation where you feel anxious, depressed, hopeless, or out of control? You probably need support. If you have been feeling this way for an extended period, are addicted to drugs, alcohol, or other vices, or are being abused or victimized emotionally, physically, or financially, you need more than just support. You need qualified, professional assistance.

If you are being abused, you should also consider legal representation in addition to professional counseling. If you do not currently have the financial resources, please investigate free resources in your area. Ask someone you truly trust and who has your best interest in mind to help you research where you can get assistance and a safe place to go if you need it. Your life, your happiness, and your safety (and the safety of your children if you have them) are too important to delay getting help.

A final note on getting support: Please do not equate the need for or use of professional assistance with weakness. The most powerful and empowering thing you can do is take a stand for yourself because *you* are worth it! Take actions that provide the support and structure for you to truly transform limiting, destructive patterns to succeed and ultimately flourish. Yes, use the Keys in this book as your guidepost. I just ask you to please find support and professional help if you are currently not strong enough, do not feel safe, or don't have the tools or ability to do this alone. I hold space for you in my heart with the highest intentions for your happiest, healthiest, safest, and most abundant, inspired life.

Rejoice in the great song of your life, and remember that while the lessons are yours, they appear as the orchestra supporting you or as the chaos controlling you.

— *DIVINITY SPEAKS*

16

KEY 12

SURRENDER

> *As you accept how your life appears now and let go of what no longer serves you, you will cherish where you currently see yourself on your path. You will know that every moment is Divinity in creation.*
>
> — *DIVINITY SPEAKS*

I have touched on surrender a few times throughout this book. Even so, surrender deserves a special seat at the table of conscious creation. Letting go of thoughts, things, relationships, or situations that keep you in the bondage of fear and negativity will help open the necessary space for the magnetic qualities of attraction energy to build. Surrender comes in many forms, and by no means implies defeat or failure. It also does not mean giving up. It is actually a very loving, courageous, and empowering thing to do when done for the right reasons. I look at surrender as letting go of something that no longer serves me. Maybe it never did serve me. Perhaps it benefited me for a little while as I tried to make it fit or pretended it still fit into my life when conditions changed, or I changed. I believe I could write a book on just this. Letting go has not always been my strong suit, especially when letting go feels scary or unknown. Thoughts, feelings, beliefs, actions, and things that are not based on the energy of love and positivity are something you may want to consider surrendering.

An example of something that may no longer serve you is the need to be right or validated. Many of us are deeply rooted in our beliefs with uncompromising minds, and we defend them with razor-sharp tongues. Most of the time, we don't even think or realize how cemented we are in our need to be right about what we hold as truth. As you learn new ways to harmonize within the energy of love and positivity, you may experience a letting go of your old self-limiting or fear-based thoughts, feelings, emotions, and belief systems. Your need to be right or to have your beliefs validated is exchanged with the grace of being open to new information in various forms. You then have a new capacity to see the world from a perspective of inner wisdom and higher truth. Additional examples of surrender include letting go of attachments to things of the physical/material world, including expectations for certain outcomes. These attachments may include things such as material possessions, people, status, health, wealth, and relationships.

We live in a world of constant change. Nothing is ever the same, even from one day to the next. It may look the same and feel the same, but the truth is, the past is only a thought. It is a memory that exists only in your mind. When you hold on to wishing something had never happened or regretting things you may have said or done, that keeps you from accepting what is. It holds you prisoner to your past, as you are unable to surrender and accept the constant changes and tremendous gifts that the continuous flow of life has to offer. When you surrender to the desire or expectation that things should stay the same or that something should happen in a specific way, you become liberated. The present moment becomes supercharged with the inspiration of your dreams, as the gifts of life flow through you. The tighter you hold on to your expectations, worry, regret, anger, or guilt, the more stuck you become in the sludge of fear energy. Letting go means going with the flow.

The reality that exists *now* is the one you are currently experiencing. The future reality that is magnetizing toward you holds unlimited potentials and possibilities. It has no agenda; it just delivers the package. When we become stagnant, when we resist change, when we condemn endings and try to desperately hold on to what used to be, we are only blocking the flow of new and wonderful beginnings within us. Letting go of *should have, could have*, and *would have* is one of the most precious gifts you can give yourself. Don't waste your energy on needless worry, guilt, anger, resentment, or regret. The Universe wants to give. It wants to serve. When you cling to the thoughts and things that no longer serve you, what does the Universe give back in return? This is not about blame, shame, or judgment, so please don't hold that belief. This is only about helping you open your inner vision so you can look beyond the finite nature of the physical world we live in. The only thing that is true, lasting, and real is the loving presence of the Universe within you and all things. All other things must one day be surrendered.

SURRENDERING TO DESIRE

Let me elaborate about surrendering to desire. Surrendering to desire isn't about asking you to stop dreaming. Dreaming, desiring, hoping, and imagining are all part of the secret of attraction energy.

Surrendering to desire may be necessary when you are too attached to a *specific* outcome or *how* that outcome should manifest; and fail to allow the Universe to give you what you need to learn, grow, or evolve. Think of it as swimming upstream instead of going with the flow. When you are not in the flow, everything is exhausting, depleting, and energetically draining. Your magnetic qualities begin to attract less than desirable outcomes as your predominant emotional and physical energy shifts. You might believe that you must continue to struggle and force outcomes to achieve your goals. Maybe you do reach a goal or outcome. Then what? It could certainly be everything you have ever dreamed of, but then what? How much of your precious time, energy, and resources have you sacrificed? How much has your health, relationships, or career suffered?

Surrendering to desire may also be necessary when you expect something in the physical world to never change or last forever. This is true whether it is letting go of a material or physical object, moving beyond the end of a relationship or career, or experiencing the passing on of a loved one. This can also be true about letting go of how something or someone used to be, including yourself. Without sounding calloused, the point is we all experience the *human condition.* We are all born into this life. We all get a chance to experience life. During this experience, we all age. We all pass from this physical life whether we want to, and whether we accept it or not. Please understand that I am not talking about negating the importance of mourning the endings in life, no matter what that ending may be. I'm not one to say, "Just get over it," and move on. We all react to endings differently, and we all need different amounts of time and levels of support to process our closures. Going through life continually dreaming about how things used to be or incessantly wishing things never changed can have dire consequences on your overall state of health, well-being, happiness, inner peace, and attraction energy. Attachments, expectations, and holding on to self-defeating desires block your ability to imagine and feel the energy of new possibilities that are waiting to be magnetized in your life.

SURRENDERING TO EGO AND BELIEF

Surrendering to ego and belief systems can be a process that evolves over time. This is probably one of the most challenging things for most people to do. Breaking patterns is not impossible, but it does take a fair amount of self-evaluation, dedication, and work. You have most likely spent your whole life identifying with yourself as your physical body. Your sense of identity is wrapped up in the form of a human with a mind that believes you are limited. Within this construct of form and function, you may have believed that hard work is what gets you to the *finish line* in life. You may believe that this is what brings the most success, fulfillment, and posterity. You may believe that self-sacrifice is paramount to achieving your goals in life and that your happiness is secondary to the happiness of others around you.

I have nothing against hard work or sacrifice for the right reasons, in the right amount, and for the right duration. When hard work and self-sacrifice become the master over your self-governing domain, you become the prisoner of your own beliefs and ego. What you once thought of as "giving it your all" turns into nothing left to give.

When you have nothing left to give, the only thing you have to hold on to is the energy of emptiness. What happens when you are on empty? Inspiration, joy, and positivity are seen as distant mountains that are too far away and too high to climb in a tired, worn out, frustrated, angry, or hopeless state of being. Surrender can be a great friend and liberator in your time of need as you release unrealistic, self-defeating expectations of yourself. You grow in courage, strength, and power as you reclaim the warrior spirit within. You regain what it takes to defend and protect your precious supply of life-force energy—the energy that you need to fill up your tank so you can optimally utilize the Keys of Conscious Creation.

I am sure by now that you see these Keys are all interrelated. The secret of attraction energy is interdependent on each Key unlocking one aspect of possibility and potential as the others remain available to use if one door gets temporarily closed. It is about slowing down and honoring yourself as the most significant guest at the table, not out of ego, but out of respect and reverence for the fact that you cannot create anything good when you are on empty.

LETTING GO

Most of us know on an intellectual level what does not serve our highest health and happiness. Habits, beliefs, lifestyles, and people can lift and support us, or become vices of self-limitation and self-destruction. If you have an idea of what you need to let go of or what needs to be changed in your life, then you have a good starting point.

Your mind may already know from an intellectual level what needs to be released or transformed, but it has not yet given you the answers that feel right or seem achievable. Otherwise, you would already have surrendered to whatever *it* is. Your heart not only knows what you need to change but how to do it. It may not have all the steps of the process, but it has answers that the mind cannot see through the darkness of fear or limitation. It is often our minds that convolute our knowing and turn it into something we are afraid of.

For instance, I once knew a woman who was being abused by her partner. It had been going on for so long that she had many excuses and explanations as to why she needed to stay in the relationship. From worry about finances, the future, her family, and what other people would think, her mind took control over her heart as she continued to convince herself that her safety, her happiness, and her pride were not important as long as she could *play the game* and try to please her partner. She began to believe her own story of unworthiness. Inevitably, the abuse continued and only became worse. She continued to cling to her mind's laundry list of why she needed to stay in the relationship. It was only after she decided to look at her life from the inside out that she realized she was not only deceiving herself, but disrespecting her very own precious gift of life.

One day, after another abusive encounter from her partner, something shifted. It was a day like any other day in which she would typically shut down, tiptoe around the obvious, and pretend everything was OK. But this day was different. She allowed herself to become present with her excuses and cover-ups and years of justifying her partner's behaviors and actions. She listened within as her heart illuminated the answer that had been hiding in the darkness of her mind. She awakened to a remembrance that her life and personal happiness was worth more than this. Despite her worry and anxiety about all of her projected fears of what might happen *if*, she looked beyond her rational mind and listened to the loving guidance of her higher self. With this newly found inner wisdom, her mind was able to work in partnership with her heart. She got the help she needed, crafted her plan, and then she bravely left the relationship. Against the brutal accusations of others who did not understand, or care to know the truth, she stepped out of the oppressive life she knew and stepped into a world filled with love, support, opportunity, and joy that received her with arms wide open. She no longer looks back, as she now looks forward to courageously living her life with a new level of joy, inspiration, peace, and purpose that was once just a distant dream.

Let me be very clear here. It was not her heart that *told* her she needed to leave the relationship. When she became present within herself and listened to her own higher wisdom, her mind was finally able to see the truth of what her heart had known for so many years. What she needed to surrender were her own feelings of fear and unworthiness and the idea that she could not survive alone. She realized and then accepted that *she was worthy* of being happy. She became present with the fact that her life was too important to waste away in the shell of a person she had become and focused on the future path on which she was surely pointed. She had been too afraid and too proud to face the truth of her abuse.

When she became present with the love and wisdom within, she announced to herself and the Universe that she was ready to stop being afraid and claim her worthiness. She was ready to live an empowered, free, and peaceful life. The Universe began to respond to the shift of her predominant energy, from fear and hopelessness to love and hope. Where she once saw obstacles and made excuses, she now saw opportunities and felt her courage. Her mind began to work in partnership with her heart to develop a plan. What once felt like roadblocks to her happiness dissolved, as what she needed to support her decision magnetized toward her in full force.

Please don't think I am telling you or anyone else to leave a relationship. Letting go of a relationship is not anything to take lightly or anything to do without serious contemplation, proper planning, and help if needed. This person had done all of that. I only use this example so you can see the power and importance of listening within before you let go. The woman, in my example, needed to let go of her own feelings of disappointing others, fear, and unworthiness so she could develop a solid plan of action and get the help she needed. If she had left the relationship without doing this, she might have questioned her decision, fallen victim to her own voice of unworthiness, not had the proper support or plan, or not been strong enough to stand in her own strength and power after the relationship ended.

We all have many types of distortions in life that do not serve us. Think about what yours may be. Perhaps you need to stop listening to fear-based or negative chatter and information in your life, whether it is outside of you or within you. Perhaps you need to slow down on social media. Maybe you need to be less judgmental of yourself or others. Maybe it's time to look at a belief you hold that is keeping you in fear or limitation. It could be time to be less enabling to people who may be taking advantage of you physically, emotionally, or financially. Maybe it's time to stop playing superman or superwoman to everyone around you. Maybe you need to let go of the story you have been carrying about yourself since childhood. What do you need to let go of or change in order to make room for inspiration, peace, prosperity, joy, hope, or healing? Do you have self-defeating or limiting habits, beliefs, or behaviors that you would like to change? Letting go of lower vibrational thoughts and feelings will open your magnetic qualities to infinite possibilities that are just waiting to flow within you. The majesty of life awaits in the castle of your own highest happiness. You are the queen or king of this magical kingdom. Claim your right to the throne!

Exercise 16
LETTING GO

Now it's your turn to go within and listen to what no longer serves you. What do you need to let go of?

- Before you begin, make sure you are in a place that feels peaceful and where you will not be interrupted.

- Start with the "Heartful Breathing Meditation" in Key 2 or whatever type of meditation works best for you. You are preparing the ground before you plant the seeds.

- Ask the Universe to open a clear channel from your higher self or higher knowing to your heart.

- Allow yourself several minutes to just flow within your meditation without expectation. The point is to allow your mind to rest as you connect with your heart.

- Placing your hands over your heart can be helpful, as you give yourself permission to *feel* the answers as they surface from within you.

- Try to be in a place of openness without expectation. When your mind begins to take control, gently acknowledge your thoughts, and then focus on your heart.

- As you deepen within your meditation, begin by gently asking your heart what no longer serves you. What might you need to do differently in life or let go of in order to unite with your joy, peace, purpose, and highest potential?

- The answers may not come immediately. Remember that you are focusing on a new way of receiving guidance from your higher self. This often comes in the language of sensation, or how you are feeling. Translating your messages into language that your mind can grasp is a process that may need to be repeated before you fully understand the messages.

- Repeat this process until you feel clear or find your own process to help you surrender to what does not serve you.

If you don't feel clear, then that may just be a sign that you need to surrender to your expectation of what clear means to you and try again without putting any pressure on yourself. In my experience, the true answers are always the ones that give me the best feeling. Feelings are the internal guidance system that can help you navigate your higher knowing and decipher the silent language within. There is a sense of clarity within the feeling and purity within the message. Don't worry if you don't perceive or feel the answers right away. When you are aligned with the energy of your highest knowing and inner peace, your love will light the way.

There is no fear on the way to love and the path of truth.

— *DIVINITY SPEAKS*

PART IV

MASTERING THE KEYS

"Let not the illusion of failure become your master. For it is here to serve you, to heal you, and to help you know the next best way of being in the reality of your choosing. Allow the illusion to flow around you like waves in the ocean. Do not fight the waves; become them. Allow them to bring you the freedom to see yourself as you truly are as you master of illusions and creator of your dreams."

— *DIVINITY SPEAKS*

17

PUTTING IT ALL TOGETHER

> *Become the greatest song of your own life, and remember that while the lessons are yours, they appear as the orchestra supporting you or as the chaos controlling you.*
>
> — DIVINITY SPEAKS

Be prepared to repeat all of the 12 Keys of Conscious Creation any time, whenever necessary, and without self-judgment. Know that these Keys are to be looked at as a process that is dynamic and ever-changing. There is really no order in which you must take them. You will learn to master some Keys more easily, and others will need revisiting. A word to the wise is not to expect perfection, for that is putting way too much pressure on yourself and isn't realistic. It took many years to become you, but it doesn't have to take years to become a new and improved you. It will take practice, effort, and commitment. If you slipped and became angry, depressed, defeated, guilty, or hopeless about a situation, let me repeat this, *please* don't beat yourself up. It's okay to be human and feel your emotional pain

—as long as you don't stay there too long. I have been there more times than I care to admit. Remember that the power of the present moment is your greatest ally, and when you focus on forgiveness and compassion or what you are grateful for in your life now, you will begin to feel your energy shift.

Transformation is a progressive process. Change can take time. When your energy begins to shift from predominantly fear-based to love-based, you will begin to notice. The wonderful thing is when others begin to notice the subtle changes as well. Yes, our egos love to be recognized. This is when I suggest wearing your knowing smile on the inside. Don't immediately discuss or brag about the changes you are experiencing. Just be your own guide around this. You don't want to set yourself up for failure due to other people's unrealistic or judgmental ideas or expectations. Your small achievements will give you just the incentive you need to keep going as you experience the outcomes of conscious creation.

As you learn to be in a state of expectancy without expectation, you avoid the disempowering energetic frequencies of uncertainty, failure, and judgment. The joyful anticipation of manifestation, whether material or related to mind, body, relationships, or spirituality, will give you the freedom to continue to express your thoughts and feelings in a positive way. Learn to become your own master on the intelligence of your heart as it begins to align with your mind.

SEE YOUR LIFE BLOOMING WITH ALL THE BEAUTIFUL COLORS OF HIGH-VIBRATIONAL ENERGY, AND THEN FEEL THE OUTCOME AS IF IT ALREADY IS. IT IS POSSIBLE FOR THE DREAM OF YOUR TOMORROW TO BE THE MASTERPIECE OF YOUR TODAY.

A FEW WORDS ABOUT NEGATIVITY

One of the questions I frequently encounter is how to manage negative opinions or influences from others as you continue on your journey of conscious creation. There is a good chance you already know the people I am talking about. They include the doubters, haters, know-it-alls, and energy suckers. I really don't like to use labels for people, so please know that these labels are meant to describe the behaviors or energies exhibited by these people, not the people themselves.

Sometimes it can be hard to remember that most people are innately pure, honest, and loving. This is especially true when you experience an action, behavior, or attitude that is completely the opposite. My husband, who is a psychic and medium, has a saying I have adopted, "There are people who do bad things; there are no bad souls".

Our souls hold the light, love, and truth of Divinity. When we incarnate into this world of form and function, we have a tendency to forget who we really are. Maybe this is by design so we can organically discover what we need to learn without interference from our higher knowing. After all, what kind of lessons would they be if we already knew all the answers?

In this classroom we call life, we each have the opportunity to learn, grow and unite with our joy, kindness, compassion, purpose, and destiny. We also have the opportunity to do the complete opposite. I would like to simply tell you to walk away, both physically and energetically, when faced with the overly emotional and sometimes hurtful, fear-based reactions that you may experience with people who do not agree with your beliefs, choices, or lifestyle. This is not always a comfortable or practical thing to do. These people are often close friends or family members, who only *mean well* with their unsolicited advice or disingenuine reactions, which is secret code that they are operating in fear-based energy. Their beliefs can represent various states of mind that reflect disempowering, self-defeating thoughts or behaviors because you are changing or doing well, and they do not understand. They may feel left behind or think you are living a more entitled life. Sometimes they feel threatened or jealous by your new outlook and accomplishments or material gains in life. Other times they just need to be right. They may be so deep down in the rabbit hole of ego, fear, anger, regret, depression, grief, and so on that your views or beliefs have to be wrong, or simply do not make any sense.

It is important to exercise a form of detached compassion for the people in your life who exhibit these behaviors. The reason I say detached is so you can discern between helping and enabling, as discussed earlier in this book. Whether they cannot see clearly through the fog of their conditioned beliefs or whether life circumstances are impeding their inner vision, it is important to remember that people *wake up* in their own time. You must remember that it is not your place to try to do it for them. I have had to revisit this a few times myself. When the remembrance of the truth of conscious creation lies dormant in the deep dream of forgetfulness, there is nothing you can outwardly do to awaken them. Your efforts may only lead to anguish, confusion, and turmoil. These are all lower-frequency, fear-based energies that do not serve you. I can't stress enough here about the importance of discernment. *Help when help is needed, and then let it go.* Whatever the reason for their behaviors, attitudes, beliefs, and actions, you will need to learn how to manage those relationships in your life if they mean that much to you. For others, you will need to decide on how to let them go physically, energetically, and emotionally.

Then, there are the energy suckers, or what I call energy vampire behaviors. Most people who exhibit this energy do not even realize what they are doing, but you know the energy I'm talking about. These are the people who leave you feeling depleted, depressed, or out of sorts just by being in their presence or engaging in a conversation. I know from personal experience that it is not always easy to avoid them, walk away, or just say goodbye. Due to my compassionate nature, I often find myself staying in their presence, just hoping that some of my good vibes will soak into them. More often than not, I am wrong, and I learned another valuable lesson to honor and trust my intuition and disengage from this depleting energy. There is often a seductive draw to engage in the perpetual dramas of this energy, as if listening to a soap opera that has the same destructive storyline with different characters for years on end. These dramas and judgments of other people or circumstances only perpetuate the low energetic frequencies of N.E.W.S. among us. And when we do get attacked for our beliefs or way of living, seemingly out of nowhere, our ego wants to defend the reason why we are right and fruitlessly try to persuade them to see our point of view or perspective. We attempt to exchange love for the disempowering, hurtful comments that are thrown at us like daggers. They may try to defend their beliefs and criticize us for the absurdity of trying to look at things in a positive light.

Just remember, you may have been there once yourself, or maybe you are there now. You may recall trying to defend your own beliefs or circumstances with so much passion that you may not have been able to see the proverbial forest through the trees. It's not your job to convert anyone to your way of knowing, or force someone to believe your personal truth. Once those around you see your positive changes and outcomes in life, they will react in one of two ways. They will be genuinely happy for you and may ask what they can do to learn more about what you did to achieve your successes, or they will exhibit negative or fear-based energy. This could be disguised by anger, jealousy, indifference, skepticism, or victim mentality. I think you understand by now what kind of energies those types of emotions are. What you need to remember is what they think about you is not your problem, and it is not your path to convince them that your way is the right way. If there is a way to help them without hurting yourself or repeating self-defeating patterns, then you be your own judge on that topic. The most powerful thing you can do is be the loving example of what is possible, while keeping your thoughts, feelings, emotions, and actions tuned to the energy of love. You will begin to see your world transform as you become your own master of manifestation.

> *Focus not on what you see but how you want your world to be.*
>
> — DIVINITY SPEAKS

THE VIBRATION OF CELEBRATION

You now hold all 12 Keys of Conscious Creation. With practice and patience, your story will unfold within the energy of love as your heart leads the way to the treasures within you. Within the powerful pull of attraction energy lies the celebration of your success. Just as each Key works together to help you magnetize and create a happier, healthier you, the vibration of celebration invites victory to the party.

CELEBRATING SUCCESS

The vibration of celebration carries the frequencies of joy, accomplishment, and fulfillment and all the subsets of this highly empowering energy. When you celebrate success, you release the energy of fear in all of its various disguises. Feelings such as doubt, despair, anger, hopelessness, anxiety, and self-judgment can easily take a back seat, as the energy of celebration confidently becomes the driving force toward your best, most fulfilled life.

The energy of celebration rides the rising tides of the ocean of possibility and potential within you. As you flow within these waves of transformation, you can feel the release of fear energy and the inner peace and clarity this brings.

REMEMBER IT IS THE RELEASE OF EVERYTHING THAT DOES NOT SERVE YOU THAT BRINGS YOU TO THE DESTINY OF YOUR DREAMS.

Give yourself praise, and celebrate your accomplishments every step of the way! Don't worry if you have to repeat some Keys due to perceived obstacles, or if some Keys take longer to learn and master than others. This is not a competition, and you are not running a race. Repeating Keys is just a reminder that you are human and that your *human* is not perfect. No one's human is perfect. But the Divine Light within you is. Allow this Light to be your guide.

Remain humble and compassionate with yourself when self-judgment, doubt, ego, or victim mentally attempt to manipulate your mind and sabotage your success. Then, recognize that just the fact you are thinking in this way is a reason to celebrate. You have identified your own perceived obstacle as you remember that you have the power, the will, and the Keys to persevere and flourish. Just because you need to pull a few weeds from your garden now and then doesn't mean it isn't beautiful, strong, healthy, and fertile. So, you pull a few weeds and plant some new seeds. Good! That is all part of planting, cultivating, and growing the healthiest, most beautiful, most bountiful, and most blissful garden of your life—the one that grows within you and then projects out to your world.

I will promise that if you keep focused on the end result of your dreams and the feeling that this brings every day, while giving thanks for the things you currently have, you will gain more reasons to celebrate your successes. The more you celebrate your successes and follow the 12 Keys of Conscious Creation, the more of what you truly dream of having, becoming, and doing will harmonize within you and actualize in your world. The Keys are within you. They always were. You just need to remember.

Exercise 17
CELEBRATE YOUR SUCCESS

This exercise will take some practice as you develop a new habit of recognizing how you think and feel about yourself, other people, things, and situations.

Remember, thoughts and feelings hold the key to unlocking unlimited possibilities in your life.

Celebrating success will likely become your favorite new habit once it becomes a part of your daily routine. It will empower you to attract and achieve greatness in all areas of your life. In order to really master celebrating your success, it will be helpful to review the energetic properties within the energy of love and fear. I suggest to write the acronyms down on a cue card or as a note in your smartphone and keep it in a place where you can reflect on them often. This way, every time you feel a certain way about yourself, another person, or a situation, you can quickly check-in and see which energy you are vibrating and attracting.

Every time you *catch* yourself in the energy of love is a reason to celebrate. And if you catch yourself in the energy of fear, this is also a reason to rejoice. Why? Because when you catch yourself in action, you have the opportunity to push the reset button. You are actually making progress toward real and lasting positive transformation just by being aware of your thoughts, feelings, and emotions. Please, do not become angry, get upset, or feel disappointed if you catch yourself in the energy of fear. This is exactly the energy you do not want to hold on to. Remember that it took a long time to become how you currently think, feel, and act. All of this has become a habitual way of being. Instead of feeling disappointed, frustrated, or angry, give yourself praise for catching yourself. Then, set your intention on how you would like to think or feel differently. You will only change your world by first changing yourself. You will only be able to celebrate your successes if you know what they are. You do this by being consciously aware of the energies you hold within the vibrations of love and fear.

NEXT STEPS

Now you have your cue card and placed it somewhere that you will look at it often. You begin to recognize when you are thinking and feeling in positive, empowering ways, and when you are thinking and feeling in negative, depleting ways. Now what? How can you celebrate things that do not seem tangible? How do you celebrate a way of thinking, feeling, and being? This is where a little creativity and fun comes in. This is your party, and you get to plan it. Celebration for one person will look different for another. I will give you some ideas to start with, but realize that you are your own best party planner. Celebration can be big or small. It really depends on how much time, effort, and enjoyment you want to put into it. This is a party for one, and *you* are the guest of honor!

The first step is always to stop and recognize the thought or feeling first. Give it a few seconds or minutes of your time. See it as something that is here to help you evolve into the grandest version of yourself—the one you have always dreamed of. Realize that it is here to help you. When you begin to see that you are noticing your thoughts and feelings, this is a reason to celebrate success. When your thoughts and feelings begin to primarily show up in the energy of love and positivity over the energy of fear and negativity, victory is celebrated. You begin to witness the amazing and magical outcomes of magnetizing your dreams.

WHAT CELEBRATION MAY LOOK LIKE:

- Take a few moments to breathe in the feeling of your success. Allow the energy of celebration to fill you with a sense of pride and accomplishment.

- Journal what you are thinking and feeling. Write something wonderful about how you recognize your success.

- Listen to some music that you might listen to when you are celebrating something. Dance, walk, run, skip, jump, or just be with the music.

- Take yourself out on a date! Do something that brings you joy. Be creative, and allow yourself to be your own best friend. If you have someone close in your life to share this celebration with, then do that. Just remember that only you may know how you truly got here, and that's okay. If you have someone in your life who knows and understands your process, then great! Sharing special moments with someone you love is a most heart-opening and connecting thing to do.

- Keep dreaming and visualizing how your success evolves. What do you see, think, and feel about how this will provide even more joy and fulfillment in your life? How will this serve your highest self and greatest good?

- Take some time to just meditate and reflect on how proud you are of yourself for learning how to attract beautiful, meaningful outcomes in your life. The journey toward mastering manifestation is a never-ending scenic route to following your heart and living your dreams.

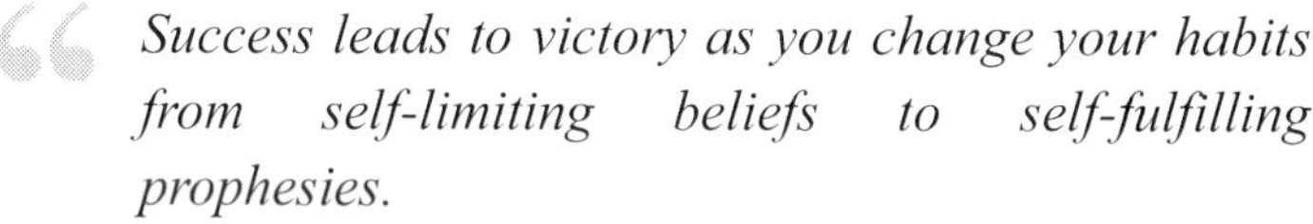

> *Success leads to victory as you change your habits from self-limiting beliefs to self-fulfilling prophesies.*
>
> — *DIVINITY SPEAKS*

18

REALIZING TRUE HAPPINESS

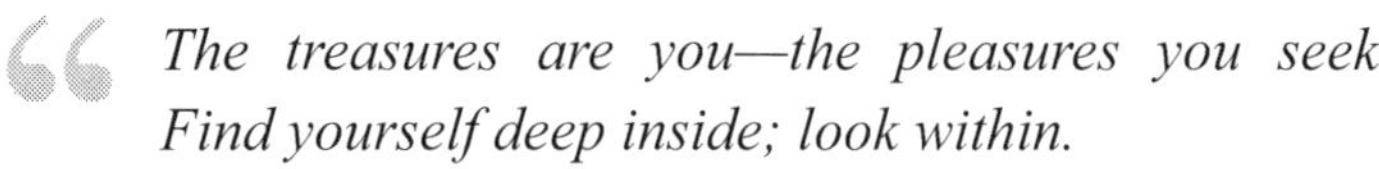

> *The treasures are you—the pleasures you seek. Find yourself deep inside; look within.*
>
> — *DIVINITY SPEAKS*

Do you ever wonder what true happiness really is? Are you curious why happiness seems to be so elusive? Here one day and gone the next, it seems to come and go on the winds of changing circumstances in our lives. It has an open invitation to indefinitely grace our lives, yet hurriedly packs its bags and leaves for unknown territory during times of pain, sorrow, and suffering.

When you reach a goal such as getting a promotion, buying something you have always wanted, doing something you have always dreamed about doing, or finding the person who makes your heart feel full, you feel happy, right? You may also feel a sense of satisfaction and completion. These are all great things to feel, but is that true happiness?

As I have said before, it is healthy and normal for our dreams to grow and change over time. You may be perfectly happy today with your current car, home, job, or hobby, but it is likely that you will eventually dream of buying a new car or move to a different home. Jobs, hobbies, and interests also change over time. Our dreams change as our desires, needs, and circumstances change. If you had a wonderful vacation, does that mean you will never want another one? There is nothing wrong with dreaming the dream of manifestation and enjoying the gifts of its bounty. It is when we identify with those outcomes and believe that the things give us true happiness that we experience the trap of attachment.

SUFFERING OCCURS WITHIN THE TRAP OF OUR ATTACHMENTS TO THE PHYSICAL WORLD.

We all know that nothing in the world is permanent. Depending on which scientific study you read, different cells in our bodies regenerate anywhere between every 1-10 years. That suffices to say that the body you are attached to today, is not the same body you had ten years ago. People come and go, jobs come and go, homes come and go, things come and go, and experiences and circumstances come and go. Nothing in our physical world is permanent, but we often forget this one basic fact of life. We tend to hold on so tightly to people, things, ideas, jobs, circumstances, lifestyles, and relationships that we become trapped in the illusion of permanence. We become trapped in the belief that happiness is dependent on what is present in our world today or what we can buy, do, achieve, or have tomorrow. Anything you have or hold may give you a sense of happiness and fulfillment today, but it will always fade with time. This is by design. Would you be happy with your first childhood toy as your only toy? Did you not wish for newer, more exciting toys as the older ones gained less appeal?

There was nothing wrong with the older ones; you just wanted more. You felt the thrill and the joy inside of you when something new came your way. I am sure this is true today as well. Toys have just changed to bigger and often more expensive objects of your desire. You fill in the blanks as to what that may be for you.

SITUATIONAL HAPPINESS

Mastering Manifestation is a tool to help you magnetize the things, experiences, people, health, wealth, and dreams you most desire. Please don't confuse the actions and outcomes of feeling situational happiness of the world with true and lasting happiness. People are born, grow older each day, and eventually pass from physical form. It is the one fact of life we cannot dispute. We rejoice when a new life is brought into the world, and we mourn when a loved one dies. We feel sad as the person we love is gone from our sight. We feel pain where we once felt pleasure.

When you lose a job that you loved, you may feel the sting of fear or uncertainty where you once felt strong and secure. You experience some level of suffering after the object of your happiness is no longer physically present in your life. This is even true with your most loved and cherished relationships. You may have relationships that last for a lifetime. But do they last for eternity? Does the physical aspect of that person in this life last forever? They will someday be gone from your physical sight.

Okay, please know that I am not trying to depress you. My only intention is to make sure I fully express what true happiness *is not* before going on to share what true happiness *is*. Hopefully, this has helped give you a chance to reflect on what happiness has meant to you up to now and how we all tend to reach for situational happiness.

TRUE AND LASTING HAPPINESS

True and lasting happiness resides within you as a pure and natural state of awareness. It does not depend on anything outside of you. It does not rely on the weather, the state of the world, who won an election, the stock market, your bank account, other people, vacations, jobs, or even good health. It transcends all thoughts, things, feelings, and emotions within the physical world. It is formless, timeless, infinite, eternal, and unchanging. It does not know pain or suffering. It does not know desire, loss, separation, or fear.

When you *look* for happiness, it means that you acknowledge that you don't have it. You feel that it is someone or something from outside of you. *Happiness is not something that can be reached; it is a state of consciousness of which you already are.* When you remember the oneness and permanent nature you share with the Divine Universe, true happiness is realized.

Do not look for happiness; simply realize that of which you are.

— *DIVINITY SPEAKS*

True and lasting happiness is found beyond the transitory, seductive, illusion of worldly situations, events, people, and things. It is realized when you detach from your desires for things of the external world. You could say that true happiness is the truth of who you are. Words are a poor representation of this extraordinary state of being. Just know that true happiness represents your true self, your true nature, and is your birthright.

In the quest for mastering manifestation, I ask you to remember the following: All worldly pleasures are temporary. They don't last. Anything from your physical world that makes you feel happy today, could feel different tomorrow. This doesn't mean that you should not enjoy them. This doesn't mean they are not important or that we should not dream or take actions for a better, happier, more fun, purposeful, and fulfilled life. I ask you to consider what it is that you are seeking and why. It is our human nature to reach for the next thing to bring us pleasure, excitement, happiness, and fulfillment. What happens when you get it or reach it? It may feel fantastic. Great! But it's temporary. You may watch a movie and laugh. You may attend a concert and feel the exhilaration of the event. You may buy a new car, the one you always hoped and wished for. What happens when the initial excitement, thrill, or joy is over? What are you left with? If you live your life in the trap of attachment to the physical plane of existence, you are left with a hole that needs to be continually filled. It's a hunger that is never satisfied. You search for the next thing to fill you up—the next thing to happen, to do, or to buy you happiness.

Having and attaining things in this world is wonderful, and I am all for it! It adds color, texture, and vibrance to the masterpiece we call life, but it is not true joy or fulfillment. True and lasting happiness only occurs as you unite with your inner bliss and awaken to your dream of remembrance. The remembrance of divine love and truth that fills all holes and heals all suffering. All life continues, all love prevails, and all beauty radiates from this Divine Illumination within you. You are you own highest happiness within the never-ending story of infinite creation.

True happiness is remembering the truth of who you are as you awaken to the Divine within.

— *DIVINITY SPEAKS*

19

THE DREAM OF REMEMBRANCE

> *Waking up to the dream of remembrance is to look beyond what you see or think you believe.*
>
> — DIVINITY SPEAKS

If you ever feel as though you are sleepwalking through life with no time to get it all done, you are not alone. Your dream of remembrance is calling you to awaken. Listen within your heart and hear the silent yet powerful voice within. The loving presence of the Universe is here to guide you to that of which you dream. It is here to say *yes* when you are in alignment with the truth of your own enlightened wisdom.

The next chapter of your life is powerfully magnetizing its way toward you with the energy of your thoughts, feelings, words, and actions. The 12 Keys of Conscious Creation can help you unlock the door to the joy, splendor, and fulfillment you have only dreamed of. Remember that just holding a key doesn't mean it will unlock the door by itself. The Keys work in unison with positivity, persistence, practice, and patience. The devotion and commitment you hold to honoring and upholding the Keys will enlighten your mind with the wisdom of your heart.

As you remember the secret of attraction energy and the 12 Keys of Conscious Creation, you are more aware of how important it is to hold the highest of peace, love, kindness, and compassion for all things, people, and situations. If negativity, judgment, division, anger, blame, and shame are your predominant energy, then life becomes magnetized toward more of the same. The hunger of these energies is never satisfied. The addicting qualities can trick you into keeping your blindfold on.

> *All you must do to remember is listen. Listen with your heart and not your mind. If you choose, the time is now for you to transcend fear, doubt, and limitation and awaken to the Truth of who you are, the actuality and expression of the Divine.*
>
> *It is up to you now as it has always been. The difference is, once you have listened within your heart to the voice of Divinity, and answered Our calls to re-balance and heal your world from the energies of fear to Love, there is much to remember, and there is no going back to sleep.*
>
> — DIVINITY SPEAKS

Look into the reality of what empathy, forgiveness, gratitude, unity, and acceptance will bring into your world. When your inner world is peaceful, loving, and still within the heart of the Universe, your outer circumstances will begin to shift.

Being open to learning new ways of self-discovery is the first step on the ladder of a never-ending journey of awakening. Don't think that just because you learn or master the Keys, there is nothing left to do or learn. It will be a process that continually unfolds and evolves. When it is time for you to stop learning in this experience we call life, you will have taken your last breath. Until then, enjoy, learn, play, sing, dance, love, inspire, and create with all the exuberance, passion, and vibrance that your mind can heartfully imagine. Don't be shy to claim your seat at the table of your highest destiny, greatest purpose, and deepest peace.

REFLECT AND PROJECT

Go back and reflect on some of the things you have awakened to within the dream of remembrance. You now have the opportunity to reflect on the inner knowing of these deep truths. Project your remembrance out into your world, and see how it radiates back toward you. Through the unseen energy of Divine Guidance, you have been led to read this book to help you remember what you already knew. This now becomes your story of how you wish to magnetize and create the life you have always dreamed of. I am just the one who helped you remember.

Along with the 12 Keys of Conscious Creation, remembering some of these highlights below will help you stay dedicated and focused within the generating, organizing, delivering energy of the divine, loving presence of the Universe.

- You have remembered that it is okay to start dreaming again. It is okay to *do you*.

- You have remembered that your life is not just one big to-do list as you awaken to the song of your soul.

- You have remembered all of the rushing through life and worrying about this and that is the exact energy you were attracting to keep you running in place and never getting anywhere.

- You have remembered to question your own beliefs and ask yourself, "Is this true?"

- You have remembered that there are no failures, only perceived obstacles that provide lessons in life, and that you can push the reset button anytime.

- You have remembered that the frequencies of love-based living and fear-based living are both equally powerful in contributing to the outcomes in your life.

- You have remembered that your emotions can be your best teachers.

- You have remembered that the present moment is like an energetic magnet. You become how you feel from one moment to the next.

- You have remembered to uphold the virtues of life and give yourself grace when you slip or forget.

- You have remembered that you can become the master of manifestation, instead of the victim of circumstance.

- You have remembered that the energy of love is P.U.R.E. It is Positive, Unifies, Regenerates, and Empowers. The energy of fear is N.E.W.S. It is Negative, Excludes, Weakens, and Separates.

- You have remembered that the energy you emit in the form of thoughts, feelings, words, and actions, greatly influence your magnetism and ultimate outcomes in your life.

- You have remembered the ingredients for attraction energy lie within the power of your inspired imagination, positive feeling, thinking, speaking, belief, and heartfelt intention.

- You have remembered that when you consciously choose to live in the energy of love and positivity versus fear and negativity, your life is happier, and you shine brighter.

- You have remembered that slowing down and listening to your heart is the best way of knowing the answers you seek.

- You have remembered that the 12 Keys of Conscious Creation are to be looked at as a process that is dynamic and ever-changing.

- You have remembered that as you develop new patterns of choosing love and positivity, over fear and negativity, you will gain the advantage of attracting the life of your dreams.

- You have remembered that it is not your job to convert others to your way of knowing. The most powerful thing you can do is to be a loving example of what is possible.

- You have remembered that you are worthy of a happy, fulfilled, peaceful, and prosperous life.

- You have remembered that true and lasting happiness resides within you as a pure and natural state of awareness. It does not depend on anything outside of you.

- You have remembered the importance of celebrating your success as you become present with how your thoughts and feelings hold the key to unlocking unlimited possibility in your life

As you reacquaint yourself with the wisdom within, keep in mind that the 12 Keys of Conscious Creation all share the stage equally. One Key is not more important than another. There is no particular order, and they are all interdependent within the energy of your higher awareness. Together, they provide a blueprint for your successful transition from the dream of forgetfulness, to awakening to the truth of who you are as the creator of your dreams.

Do you remember what I said at the beginning of this book about reserving your judgment until the end? How do you feel about knowing that failure is just another opportunity to practice the secret of attraction energy as you learn, grow, and try again? If you have made it this far, my guess is that you are no longer just intrigued or hopeful, but *positive* that you can do this. Even if you are only pretty sure, that is a starting point. I know without a doubt that you can hear the song of your soul and feel the dreams of your destiny as you wake up from the deep sleep of forgetfulness. You have the potential to do this and more. We all do!

THE ENERGY OF ALLOWING

My suggestion is when you decide to proceed, don't try but allow. Trying implies something that has not yet happened and may never happen. Trying perpetuates the energy of possible doubt, as it signals your subconscious that you have not yet received or created the outcome yet. This leads to a perpetual loop of trying to obtain or trying to become something that remains somewhere or sometime off in the future.

ALLOWING IS THE SILENT, YET POWERFUL ENERGY FROM WITHIN THAT KEEPS YOU CONNECTED TO THE FLOW OF YOUR DIVINE POTENTIAL.

Allowing enables the perpetual energy and power of the present to help you master manifestation as you become the awakened dreamer you were always meant to be. Allowing opens the portal to your inspired imagination to magnetize the life of your dreams in unison with the secret of attraction energy.

Focusing on fear and negativity, living in the past and reliving pain, suffering, loss, or regret, significantly impedes the flow of your remembrance of the truth of who you are and the extraordinary potentials waiting within you. As you advance in your practice of allowing through persistence and patience, you will begin to transcend allowing to knowing, which is the language of the absolute. Once you begin to know, you will become your own masterpiece within the heart of your imagination and the canvas of your creation.

Now is your time to *know* that the outcomes of your personal world are built on the keys of your own repeating patterns of belief, thought, and emotion. If your predominant energy is focused on the repeating patterns of fear and negativity, you will experience a vastly different life than one predominately based on the energy of love and positivity. As you begin to remember the truth of who you are—a being of unlimited potential—the magnetic energy of love and positivity will grow stronger. Your life will begin to show you the evidence of your mastery, as you allow the higher vibrational energies to be your guide. Practice the Keys in this book with excitement and enthusiasm. You have the tools and ability to think, imagine, *and* feel the deepest desires of your dreams come true. The proper actions and outcomes will follow when they align with the goals of your heart.

Again, my recommendation is to keep a journal because this can happen fast. When your reality switches from negative-based and fear-based to one of positive-based and love-based, you may not realize you have made the transition because your old self is no longer who you are. I have been keeping journals on and off for more than forty years. I can't tell you how many different versions of me I read about when I go back in time and read some of my entries. In some of those entries, I am so far disconnected from my current reality that the old me feels like a distant dream. From the basis of measuring your success and seeing your growth, it is nice to have some sort of a journal as a baseline from where you started.

A final note on love-based versus fear-based reality. I must reiterate that when I reference living in a fear-based reality, this in no way implies that you do not love, that you do not feel love, or that you are not a good person. This is merely the term representing all the energy and feelings that occur in a fear, limitation, or negativity-based view of yourself or the world.

When less than empowering thoughts and feelings dominate, the perception of your current reality is based on separateness over unity and stagnation over creation. Fear-based thinking and feeling ultimately create the opposite (or unfulfilled outcomes) of your highest desires, goals, or life purpose.

The pathway to attracting and creating the life of your dreams is by aligning yourself with the frequency of love, and then calling on your inspired imagination as you maintain these thoughts and feelings of the heart. When you remember this, and consciously choose to have your thoughts and feelings based on love, peace, gratitude, compassion, truth, forgiveness, acceptance, joy, tolerance, and unity, your vision of yourself and the world is seen and experienced through the eyes of beauty, and from the heart of the Divine.

Now, I will ask you this: Are you ready to awaken from the dream of forgetfulness and dance to the song of your soul? Is it time to begin mastering your own manifestations from this melody? Are you ready to attract and live the life of your dreams?

Proclaim your I-am.

Proclaim the truth of your song within the harmonizing vibrations of love and the inspiration of your imagination.

Sing it into existence with exuberance, persistence, and faith.

And say it is so.

> *As you choose to think, you shall be. As you choose to feel, you shall see. Speak this into existence with the Love of your heart and the devotion of your Soul. Awaken to the dream of remembrance. Awaken to the Truth of who you really are.*
>
> — DIVINITY SPEAKS

DIVINITY SPEAKS

This epilogue is dedicated to two inspired messages from Divinity, which provided the foundation for writing *Mastering Manifestation*.

THE HIGHEST TRUTH

The world as a whole is a collective reflection of your individual light. The more you chose to practice love and non-judgment of others in all regards, the brighter your individual lights shine and reflect out into the world.

The brighter lights bring harmony and healing and a sense of hope, purpose, and joy.

When shades of fear are painted into the hearts of humans, their lights shine dimmer and only reflect that of which they fear. It is often an unconscious choice, but yet it is still a choice.

You have the capacity to awaken into the light of

Love and leave the bondage and deception of fear behind you.

Anything divided is false and not of Love.

Love is the only truth and the only way to find complete renunciation of the fiction in the hearts of humankind. For the story of fiction was planted long ago, and the seeds of this story have grown into weeds which strangle the harvest of your bounties on earth.

The natural rights you have as humans to control your own destiny and create your own reality have always been available.

Current shades of reality are manifested in the grips of fear, judgment, control, and division. This is not the reality your hearts of Light and Love would choose.

As you begin to unite instead of divide, your purpose of reclaiming your world grows stronger in energy and numbers.

As you begin to turn away from mass programming, you begin to remember the truth of who you are as beings of the Light and masters of the land.

Keeping yourself protected from the false information in your collective programming is not the same as being ignorant. For true knowledge is received by the hearts of humans and is not something that is taught, watched, or learned. It is the capacity to merge your own consciousness with Divine Consciousness and then remember that the individual is also the collective.

Wherever you are, there I AM, and I AM the Light, the Love, the Beauty, and the Truth of what is real, eternal, and accessible to everyone.

Go into your days with hope, joy, and renewed purpose in your hearts. Leave the story of fear behind, and join your true destiny with a renewed sense of being Love.

As you remember Love, you remember unity. As you remember unity, you remember the dream of awakening into the truth of your indivisible connection with Me.

There is never a moment in your life in which you do not have access to this and do not have access to the destiny of your most fulfilling desires.

Our hearts are One, and Our purpose is great. Do not waste your purpose on ugliness, deception, control, and division. Unite as you were meant to unite and awaken from the slumber of deception into the truth of reality.

Know that every light that shines brighter contributes to the reflection of the whole and the healing of your world.

— *DIVINITY SPEAKS*

HOW TO ATTRACT THE OUTCOMES IN LIFE YOU MOST DESIRE

The flow of life within the timelessness of eternity is how you feel it to be and how you believe it to feel.

The less inner restrictions or limitations of mind and heart, the more ease you will feel. You begin to unite with the infinite possibilities of positive outcomes already within you. Peace, clarity, joy, and prosperity flow through the movement of Source Energy within the infinite field of you.

How do you remove or transform these inner restrictions or perceived limitations to attract the outcomes you most desire in life? It begins with a desire but ends with a belief. Many do not have the belief that the desire is possible.

Transforming belief begins with an activation process within your own imagination. It begins with challenging what you think you already know or believe to hold true.

As a thought begins to build, the mind has the ability to shape the thought, which then has a corresponding feeling. Merge the thought and the feeling of your desire fulfilled through the eyes of your imagination. The more you heartfully practice this, the inner restrictions of mind and heart become unblocked. They become free to unite with new moments within the field of intention and possibility.

Your belief will transform into a new possibility as the imagination lights the way to your desires through the flow of Source Energy within.

The course of life is how you feel it to be and how you believe it to feel. Do not allow the course of your life to be dictated by the memories or feelings of your past or worry of the future. These moments in timelessness are objectified by the concentration of your memories and the strength of your emotion. They magnetize outcomes in your life in ways beyond the understanding of your conscious mind. They attract the outcomes you least desire.

Suffering lies in the attachment to your expectations and beliefs. When you move beyond your attachments, you unite within the flow of The Universe and accept that Reality is the life that flows through all things seen as good, bad, and indifferent. Your part in this Reality is to be true to your destiny as you listen within to the song of your Soul.

— *DIVINITY SPEAKS*

ABOUT THE AUTHOR

Shannon MacDonald is a bestselling author, spiritual channel, and ascension guide with years of experience pioneering the field of spiritual awakening and higher consciousness communication. Her books, services, and events serve as gateways to higher healing, enlightened living, and conscious creation.

Shannon's expertise lies in helping others raise their frequency and access higher awareness, enabling them to break free from limiting beliefs, unlock their greater purpose, and actualize their highest potentials. Her unique ability to channel Ascension Frequencies has transformed countless lives, fostering profound spiritual growth and healing across past, present, parallel, and multidimensional lifetimes.

During her fulfilling career as a registered nurse, Shannon discovered her innate calling as a healer. She observed significant reductions in physical and emotional pain, along with profound and unexpected healing, when applying energetic healing techniques. This realization led her to delve deeper into energy healing, mastering various modalities such as Reiki, Spiritual Healing, Reconnective Healing, and Quantum Healing.

Living in Florida with her husband and their cherished German Shepherd, Shannon values time spent with loved ones, exploring nature, cycling, and enjoying motorcycle rides. Her life's work is devoted to helping others elevate their consciousness and create positive shifts in their lives. Shannon offers exceptional guidance and support for those seeking a more meaningful, purposeful, and enlightened existence.

Visit Shannon online to learn more:
ShannonMacDonald.net

MORE FROM SHANNON

If you enjoyed this book and feel like it gave you some value, I would greatly appreciate a review on Amazon. I am a self-published author and don't have a marketing team behind me. What I have is YOU!

Follow me on YouTube for inspirational messages and guided meditations to help support your spiritual awakening, deepen your peace, and rise above the programs of a conditioned reality.

youtube.com/@ShannonMacDonaldAuthor

Sign up for my mailing list to receive early notifications on my upcoming books and events!

ShannonMacDonald.net/sign-up

Thank you! Your support means a lot to me.

ALSO BY SHANNON MACDONALD

Navigating Ascension Symptoms

A Guide to Spiritual Awakening and Higher Healing

This power-packed, quick-read book demystifies the ascension process and equips you with practical tools to navigate the cosmic rollercoaster of ascension symptoms with clarity and confidence.

Free Download on Shannon's website
or buy the print and ebook on Amazon

ShannonMacDonald.net/all-books

New Earth Reality

The Other Side of Ascension

The Great Liberation

Sequel to New Earth Rising

As humanity approaches The Great Liberation and Ascension to the New Earth, *The Other Side of Ascension* continues with vital questions for humanity to consider and new information to absorb regarding The Great Liberation of human consciousness and the next sitting of Reality.

ShannonMacDonald.net/the-other-side-of-ascension-book

New Earth Rising

Starseed Transmissions for Awakening, Activation, and Ascension

Channeled messages revealing Earth's hidden history, cosmic origins, and the true nature of Reality and Ascension.

Awaken higher awareness, activate dormant consciousness and liberate from false reality programs that steal our free will and hijack our conscious evolution.

ShannonMacDonald.net/new-earth-rising-book

Breaking Free

Unfollow the Fear, Unplug from the Programs, Unsubscribe from the Propaganda

Learn How to discern TRUTH in information, facts over fallacy, and find freedom from fear. A book for Awakened Living.

Discover how you can liberate your mind and have clear access to paradigm-shifting ideas and life-transforming truth about reality.

ShannonMacDonald.net/breaking-free-book

I Am She

Positive & Empowering Affirmations for Women to Awaken and Celebrate the Divine Feminine and Sacred Heritage of the Goddess Within

A beautifully illustrated affirmation book to guide women on a journey of deep self-discovery of their true and radiant nature as The Goddess.

I Am She is a cherished keepsake for women of all ages. Enchanting full color illustrations with each affirmation.

ShannonMacDonald.net/i-am-she-book

The No News Diet

Detox from Information Overload

A healthy diet doesn't just include the quantity and quality of food you put into your mouth. It also includes the ideas and information you put into your mind.

Learn how to detoxify from the effects of informational overeating and reset your energetic microbiome to a happier, healthier, more hopeful place.

ShannonMacDonald.net/the-no-news-diet-book

Made in United States
Orlando, FL
18 October 2024

52747599R00122